PREPARE YOUR HOME FOR A SUDDEN GRID-DOWN SITUATION

TAKE SELF-RELIANCE TO THE NEXT LEVEL WITH
PROVEN METHODS AND STRATEGIES TO SURVIVE A
GRID-DOWN CRISIS

TED RILEY

CONTENTS

A Special Gift to My Readers

Included with your purchase of this book is your free copy of the *Emergency Information Planner*

Follow the link below to receive your copy:
www.tedrileyauthor.com
Or by accessing the QR code:

You can also join our Facebook community **Suburban Prepping with Ted**, or contact me directly via ted@tedrileyauthor.com.

INTRODUCTION

"Remember: When disaster strikes, the time to prepare has passed."

— STEVEN CRYOS

Picture the scene: The whole family's snuggled up on the sofa watching a movie, and the kids are wolfing down popcorn like there's no tomorrow. The heating's on, the lights are glowing, and you're considering hot chocolate all around. Then suddenly, the TV screen is black, the lights are off, the heating's cut out, and boiling water for hot chocolate has become a serious mission. Plus the kids have lost the plot, and your wife's panicking about how you're all going to navigate the morning routine.

That was my house a couple of weeks ago.

It was all totally fine—over within a few hours, in fact. It was just a short-term power outage; no doubt you've had them yourself. And if you're anything like me, you've got everything you need to handle them. We actually had a good evening. Once the kids had calmed down, we filled the front room with candles, wrapped ourselves in blankets, and cracked open the board games. And we made that hot chocolate over a camping stove, found in the back of a cupboard with the help of a flashlight. The kids loved it. Arguably we had a better night than we would have had watching the movie.

It got me thinking though. We were fine for a few hours. We had everything we needed to see us through an immediate problem with the grid… But would we have coped if it had gone on for weeks? The answer, unfortunately, was no. We'd have been fine for a little while, but if we had to live without power for more than a couple of weeks, we'd have struggled.

There have been disasters and power outages all across America over the last few years, and the same is true in Europe, Asia, and Oceania. The problem isn't getting better. In fact, it's only getting worse. We're facing more and more extreme weather, and the grid is subject to increasing pressure. The chances of a longer-term grid-down situation are becoming ever more likely.

That small-scale power outage made me realize: We need to be more prepared. And if my family, a family for whom being prepared is second nature, needed to work on this, how many other families would struggle if the grid was to go down?

And this, I know, is why you're here.

We're all afraid that we won't be able to keep our families safe and healthy if the comforts we currently rely on suddenly become unavailable. Most of us are fully dependent on the grid, and if you're wondering how you'd cope without it, you're certainly not alone. We haven't had to think about how to meet the demands of a busy household without it, so most of us haven't. You might not be aware of what equipment you need to have in backup, how you'll keep up with your family's personal hygiene and medical needs, what you'll do about cooking, or how you'll communicate with the outside world. You might have worried about what you'll do if you get caught without power, but are you equipped for it? Do you even fully understand what it means?

Perhaps, like me, a power outage woke you up to the fact that you need to be more prepared, or perhaps you were taking stock of the supplies you've already prepared for a disaster, only to realize that all that rice isn't going to be much use without a way to cook it. You're looking for solutions, and let me tell you, you've come to the right place. Once I get a whiff of a hole in my own preparedness plan, I'm obsessive, so I can tell you I've thought all this through thoroughly.

You're going to come away with practical advice you can implement straight away to make sure your family's prepared no matter what happens. You'll have a clear idea of the essential supplies you'll want to get hold of in case we find ourselves faced with a grid-down emergency, and you'll have a better understanding of the bases you need to cover. You'll learn strategies that will help you in a range of different disasters, and you'll recognize exactly what you currently rely on the grid for so that you're better equipped to think around it.

I've spent years studying wilderness and urban survival, and my family and I have been preparing our homestead for the worst for years. I might have left a few gaps in my original plan, but we're on it now, and I promise you can trust the information I'm going to share with you. If wilderness survival is possible, then urban survival is possible—even without the grid. In fact, there are plenty of people who live off the grid by choice. I read about one man in Florida who's been living in a camper van, completely independent from the grid, for 20 years. He's going to be fine if the grid goes down... But don't worry: It won't be long before you will be too.

Those short-term power outages will be a piece of cake, but better yet, you'll be ready to face something much more serious. I've taken all the hard work out for you: You don't have to think about a thing. Just assess your family's needs, gather your supplies, and stock up. And you might want to practice a few things too, but don't worry: We'll get to that.

So let's not waste any more time. Let's make sure we're ready for whatever the world wants to throw at us next. Preparedness is a journey, and this is the next step on the path to surviving comfortably, no matter what.

1

WHEN THE GRID GOES DOWN

WHAT IT MEANS FOR YOU

What comes to mind when you think of the grid going down? The chances are it's something like my recent power outage. You may think of a time without lights, heating, and cooking facilities; you probably realize that hot water and laundry are going to be an issue. But a true grid-down scenario has a far greater impact than most people realize. Let's take a step back for a second and think about the kinds of events that could cause a grid-down scenario. I think if you're to be truly prepared, it's important to think about cause as well as effect.

POTENTIAL CAUSES OF PROLONGED GRID FAILURE

My aim isn't to go into a lot of depth about each of these potential disasters. It's simply to help you build an awareness of the sorts of things that could affect the grid. In my experience, most people are aware of the physical consequences of many of these things, but imagining a life without power is so alien to us that many people overlook it.

The most obvious causes of grid failure are natural disasters and environmental events. At the minor end of the scale, that's regional weather; at the extreme end, it's tsunamis, floods, and earthquakes. Generally speaking, regional weather events are less likely to affect the grid for a prolonged period of time. However, an intense storm or a tornado could cause significant damage to a distribution system, and it could mean an area is without power for a while. With an event like an earthquake, there's even greater potential for disruption. Transmission poles, distribution poles, and substations are all vulnerable to damage, and there's a significant risk of fuel loss. Flooding, ice storms, volcanic activity, wildfires, and drought can also cause great damage, and the problem with all of these weather events is that as the climate warms, they become much more likely to occur in areas where the infrastructure isn't prepared for them.

Extreme weather on Earth isn't the only risk to the grid, though. What happens in space also affects our environment. Storms on the sun, for example, cause eruptions of charged particles known as coronal mass ejections, and these can result in fluctuations in the Earth's magnetic field. There's a lot of science we could go into here, but the simple story is that these fluctuations can damage the whole power system. And unfortunately, coronal mass ejection isn't the only space event that can impact the magnetic field here on Earth.

Much as we may like to think that all threats to the grid are natural occurrences, sadly, this is not the case, and we are at the mercy of deliberate interference too. Terrorist attacks and cyberattacks are a risk, and even if the grid is not an intentional target, war and conflict can also have devastating effects. Many of us are lucky enough not to be affected by these things in our daily lives, but the harsh reality is that life can change in an instant, and we should be prepared for every possibility.

WHAT WOULD HAPPEN IF THE GRID WENT DOWN?

If any of these events did shut down the grid, the impact would be immense. There are 3 things we rely on to function day-to-day: food, water, and money. All of these things would be affected. Water supplies would shut down without the grid to power them. Backup generators would keep them going for a while, but there's a limit, and it wouldn't be long before the faucets would run dry and the sewage system would back up. Access to food, meanwhile, would become much more difficult. Many producers rely on automated services, which would cease to function without power. Refrigeration and delivery would be impossible, and even if delivery trucks could run, stores would soon be unable to keep up with demand, and the shelves would empty quickly. And for us at home, refrigeration, preparation, and cooking would all require an emergency backup plan to be in place.

Money may seem like less of a necessity in this context, but the world revolves around it, and in our current system, we need it in order to access goods and services. We live in an increasingly cashless society, and that means our ability to use money is almost entirely dependent on electricity.

These are perhaps the most significant problems, but they're not the only ones. In a large-scale grid-down situation, the gas supply would run out, cell phone service would cease, mail wouldn't be delivered, and schools would close. It isn't as simple as the lights going off. Life as we know it would be altered dramatically.

In the worst-case scenario, there's a real risk of civil unrest and a high chance that martial law would be enforced. If things were to get this bad, everyone would be focused on surviving and keeping their families safe—at all costs. Even emergency workers and those we rely on to uphold the law would be forced to work for service rather than pay, and understandably, many would choose to prioritize their families. The services we rely on to protect us would be understaffed and strained in the face of rising crime levels, which is bound to happen if people become desperate.

I bring this up not to instill fear, and indeed, I would give anything for this never to happen. But I think being prepared means being aware of the worst eventualities and making sure you can survive no matter what happens outside.

REMEMBERING YOUR SURVIVAL PRIORITIES

I'm conscious that many of you will have read my previous book, *When Crisis Hits Suburbia*, and I want to avoid rehashing old ground. However, it's natural that there will be overlaps, and when we're thinking about survival there are 6 key priorities that you need to take care of. These are food, water, medicine, security, energy, and hygiene, and thriving in a grid-down situation means ensuring that these priorities are met. The areas we'll look at over the coming chapters will cover these necessities, so you don't need to worry, but I would advise keeping them in the back of your mind at all times. When you're forced to think outside of the box, it's important to stay focused on the most important details.

A grid-down situation would leave us without the things we take for granted for a longer period of time than a simple power outage. It could be short-term (think 4 to 6 weeks), or it could go on for much longer. While it may be less likely, and while we may hope that it never comes to this, we need to be prepared to cope if it happens. There's great peace of mind in that, I think, and I hope that by the end of this book, you'll share that peace of mind with me.

2

THE POWER'S OUT!

IMMEDIATE SHORT-TERM SOLUTIONS

The recent power outage was no problem for my family because we already had everything on hand to see us through. The kids came home from school the next day, however, with stories of classmates who had struggled more. One family, apparently, had no alternative lighting apart from the lights on their phones; another had been in the middle of cooking dinner and hadn't been able to finish the process. So I want to start with the basics and make sure we have the first moments of a grid-down situation or a very short-term power outage covered. From there, we can start thinking about how we can build on that in order to prepare for a more serious situation.

ESSENTIAL POWER OUTAGE SUPPLIES

I hope it never gets more serious than the occasional power outage, but I suspect that at the very least, we're going to see an increase in these over the coming years. Preparing for them is relatively simple, though, and even if you haven't thought about this before, you'll probably find that you already have a lot of what you need on hand.

Flashlights and Headlamps

The first place I'd start is with flashlights. It might seem obvious, but now that we rely on our phones so much, you'd be surprised by how many people no longer have them. I'd make sure you have something long-lasting that can withstand low temperatures and is waterproof. Think long-term: If you end up in a more serious situation due to extreme weather, you want to make sure all your gear can withstand the conditions. There are hundreds of options out there, but I'll give you a couple of good starting points. I have both of these, and I've only had good experiences with them so far.

Fenix PD36R: Waterproof, dustproof, and shock-resistant, this one lasts up to 115 hours. It needs charging though, so if the power was out for a long time, you'd need to be able to charge it from a backup power source.

Olight Warrior Mini 2 EDC Tactical Light: This one ranks well for durability. It's extremely waterproof and will last for about 164 hours. This model is battery-powered, but the battery can be recharged within the device.

I'd also recommend having at least one headlamp, but there's a good argument for everyone in the family having one. When you need to find your way around the house in the dark, having your hands free is a definite bonus, and if you're also dealing with the aftermath of a disaster, it's going to be essential. Again, there are hundreds of options on the market, but if you're not sure what to look for, this is what I have, and I can definitely recommend it.

Black Diamond ReVolt 350: Switched to low mode, this model has a 200-hour battery life, and enables you to see for over 260 feet. It has a night vision function, it's waterproof, and it has multiple settings for different purposes.

Food and Water

Government recommendations are to have enough food and water to keep each member of the household going for 72 hours. That means 1 gallon of water each per day for 3 full days. That's just for drinking though, and if the water isn't running, you'll need more than that for bathing and cooking. If you're starting from nothing though, these guidelines are a good place to begin, and it is likely that, for a short-term outage, you'll only need to get through a few hours.

When it comes to food, there are whole books you could write on the subject (I should know: I've written one!), but the short story is that if the power's out for more than a few hours, you're going to want to avoid opening the refrigerator as much as possible, and if it goes on for longer than that, you want to make sure you have food that won't spoil. Take a look at my last book, *The Prepper's Pantry* for a more comprehensive look at food stocking and storage. If you have pets, remember you'll need food for them too.

As for keeping food fresh short-term, I find it helpful to think of a power outage as being like a camping trip. If you think of it as camping from home, it's pretty easy to think about the kind of supplies you might want, and one of those things is a cooler. If your fridge is out of action, that'll ensure that your milk and other staples stay fresher for longer.

First Aid and Medication

The chances of someone getting injured aren't much more likely in a short-term power outage than they are in your normal life, but you should really have a first aid kit on hand anyway. You just never know. We'll take a closer look at medical care in Chapter Eight, but at the very least, make sure you have a basic first aid kit in your house. I'd also recommend having a stock of any prescription medications your family needs. Short term, it's probably not an issue, but if that power outage turns out to be something bigger, you're going to want these.

Alternative Lighting

Flashlights and headlamps will only get you so far. If the power's out even for just an evening, you don't want to have to sit around all night holding a flashlight. I'd recommend having a few battery-operated lanterns. You could also use oil lanterns or candle lanterns, or you could have a mix of all 3. Personally, we have all of them, although the candle lanterns, I must confess, are mostly because my wife likes to have them around anyway. She likes to hang them in the garden on a summer's evening, and she's not wrong: It makes the whole place look magical. If you could use a little help with choosing battery-operated lanterns, here's my favorite. I only have one of these at the moment, but I'd definitely consider getting a couple more.

Streamlight Super Siege: This is a bit extra in terms of the features it offers, but if it came to a long-term outage, I'd say it's worth the investment. It will last for 36 hours on the lowest setting and includes red LEDs for night vision. It has a rechargeable battery, so you'd need backup power long-term, and it's waterproof, so it will survive harsh weather. In fact, it even floats, so if you were to find yourself in a flood situation, it's possibly the best option you could have.

They might feel a bit retro in comparison, but I'd recommend having a good supply of candles too. Obviously, you'd need them for candle lanterns anyway, but they're a good extra for lighting rooms at night. Be careful about the candles you buy though. Don't bother with fancy dinner candles. They burn quickly, and you'll go through them fast. Go for an emergency candle—you can get them to last for up to 115 hours. Bear in mind that you'll need a good supply of lighters and matches too, especially if you'll also be lighting gas stoves for cooking.

Power

Even for a short-term power outage, you're going to want to have spare batteries on hand. That flashlight is useless if the batteries die halfway through the outage. I have a list of all the different types of batteries I need for specific emergency items so that I can be sure I have enough in stock. If any of your devices require a screwdriver to get into the battery compartment, keep this nearby so you can easily execute a battery change if needed. I'd recommend having portable phone chargers too. Make sure they're always fully charged so that if the power does go out for an evening, you still have access to at least one phone. A longer-term problem might be a different matter, but short term, you'll still have internet access, and having your phone will mean you can access information about the situation and contact anyone you need to. That said, I'd recommend having a weather radio in your emergency kit too. That way, you can still access updates if all else fails. You can get battery-operated ones, solar-powered ones, and hand-crank ones, and many double up as chargers, so they're well worth the investment.

Cooking

As far as a short-term problem goes, again, think camping. A camping stove is a good idea, even if the power's only out for a night. Remember my son's friend whose family didn't have a way to finish cooking the evening meal? If they'd had a camping stove, they wouldn't have had a problem. Remember you'll also want to have a couple of backup gas canisters on hand, and you'll need the appropriate cookware to use with your stove. I'm not going to go into a lot of detail about your options for camping stoves here, but we'll go deeper in Chapter Seven when we look at food and cooking. A thermos is a good idea too —you can't reheat anything in the microwave if the power's out, so a way to keep your food warm is a good idea, not only for ease but also for conserving power.

Bathroom Help

There are a couple of emergency items that not many people think of when it comes to short-term outages. Bear in mind that if your power's out, your toilet's not going to flush. Therefore, a bucket is a good idea. You can just avoid flushing some of the time, but not to put too fine a point on it, even in the space of an evening, there are times that you're going to want to flush, and if you have enough water in stock, you can use it for this if you have a bucket. You'll also want some hand sanitizer to cover you if your water's off.

Staying Warm, Cool, and Entertained

Whether you'll need to keep warm or keep cool when the power's off will depend on where you live, the time of year, and the reason for the power outage, but the chances are you could need provisions for either. For staying warm, make sure everyone in the family has an insulated sleeping bag, and keep a supply of cozy blankets on hand too. For staying cool, a battery-operated fan is a good idea, and you could even keep a supply of the old-fashioned manual type handy.

Lastly, remember that if the power's out, you've lost access to TV, video games, and web surfing. Especially if you have children, you want to have some power-free entertainment on hand. Books are a good option, but I also like the opportunity to bring the family together, particularly if people are uneasy or panicking. Board games, card games... Whatever you like. Just make sure you have something to while away the powerless hours.

WARM WEATHER POWER OUTAGE TIPS

If you live in a warm climate, or it's a warm time of year where you live, you'll need to factor this into your emergency planning. Your family's water needs are greater when it's warmer, so I'd up the one gallon each per day to two to be on the safe side. Think about the amount of heat generated by your light sources too. Candles, gas lanterns, and oil lamps will produce more heat than battery lanterns, and solar lamps are a good option too.

If you live in a warm region, you probably rely on air conditioning, and that won't be running if the power's out. To keep yourself cool, pay particular attention to hydration, drinking even if you're not feeling thirsty. Be cautious about alcohol and caffeine, as they dehydrate you, and you end up eliminating more water than you gain.

Keep the air moving by opening windows in the morning and evening, ideally on either side of a room to create a through draft. Keep them closed during the middle of the day though: At the hottest part of the day, opening the windows will only bring warm air inside. Make use of battery-powered or solar fans to keep the air circulating, and consider positioning one by the window to push warm air out and draw cooler air in. Even if you have the fan in the middle of the room, keeping the windows open will help you maintain a cross breeze. A final tip for keeping a room cool, which was given to me by a friend in the Philippines: Try hanging a damp towel in front of your fan. Easy DIY cooling system!

Wear light, comfortable clothes around the house, and when night falls, if you find it's too hot to sleep, try dampening your top sheet. You don't want to sleep with damp fabric against your skin, but if you use a top sheet, it will draw the heat out and help you sleep more comfortably.

When it comes to food, it might be a good idea to have supplies that don't require much, if any, cooking. The more cooking you need to do, the more you're going to heat your home. For a short-term outage, when you still have plenty of fresh food on hand or it's easy to get out for supplies, consider grilling outdoors to keep all the extra heat outside of the house.

As for your frozen and refrigerated provisions, unfortunately, they're going to warm up and spoil much more quickly in warm conditions. If you have backup power, you can keep your fridge and freezer running, but if not, you can prepare to keep food fresher for longer by filling empty spaces in the freezer with jugs or bags of water. This will help to stabilize the temperature and give your stocks a little extra life. Just be sure to leave enough room in the containers for the water to expand as it freezes. Another alternative is to get hold of some dry ice if you can, which will keep you going a little longer.

If you're without power for more than a couple of days, your frozen goods will start to perish. Eat the most sensitive things first (your kids won't be averse to helping out with the ice cream). If you need to save meat, fruits, or vegetables, you can set about preserving them. There's plenty of guidance for this in *The Prepper's Pantry*.

COLD WEATHER POWER OUTAGE TIPS

On the opposite side of the coin, if you live in a colder region, you're probably used to relying on central heating, and this won't be available to you if the power goes down. The first thing I'd recommend is to secure your property as much as you can to prevent it from losing heat. Common entry points for cold air are around the kitchen extraction fan and dryer vent, the gaps around windows and doors, the fireplace and chimney, the vents around the water heater and furnace, and any external wall outlets. You can reduce heat loss in these areas by sealing the leaks around the windows and doors with painter's tape, and stuffing gaps with rolled-up towels. You can also insulate the windows without sacrificing light by covering them with clear plastic sheeting.

With heat loss kept to a minimum, you can then begin to create microclimates in your home so that you have one area that's warmer than the rest of the house. One idea is to set up an indoor tent. It's slightly off-the-wall, I agree, but the added insulation is surprisingly effective, especially when you have several bodies in there creating heat. Alternatively, you could build a blanket fort. Get the kids involved in that one—they'll love it! To conserve fuel and encourage the microclimate ethos, try to keep most of your family's activity to one room. You can block drafts under the door with rolled-up blankets, and warm the room with a wood stove or alternative heat source (we'll look more closely at that in Chapter Four).

Clothing-wise, think layers. You want a base layer first, which will wick moisture away from the skin. Synthetic fabrics are a good choice for this. Follow this with a middle layer, which will add insulation and help your body retain heat. Flannel shirts and woolen sweaters are good choices. Top it all off with an outer layer, which is more important if you're going to be outside and exposed to the weather, but which will add extra warmth if you're struggling to maintain your body temperature indoors. A jacket or a thick hoodie are good options. Dress warmly from the moment you get up, and remember to cover your head to prevent heat loss, and protect your extremities (think gloves and thick socks). You can warm yourself up from the inside out too. Drink warm fluids and eat warming foods. As long as you have backup cooking options, this shouldn't be a problem.

Movement is also good for warming you up. A 20-minute exercise session can keep you warm for an hour, and you don't need to make it a formal workout. Play with the kids, dance, do jumping jacks... Do anything you like as long as you're moving and bringing up your body temperature.

Of course, you won't want to be on the move all day. In the evening, snuggle up in blankets and sleeping bags, sharing body heat with your family. Hot water bottles and brick warmers are a good idea too.

Lastly, when you're building your emergency stockpile, you'll want to pay particular attention to fuel. Make sure you have enough wood, gas, or whatever else you'll burn when the power's off to see you through at least a few days.

These tips will see you through a short-term outage and get you started in the immediate moments of a grid-down scenario. However, a full knock to the grid could take much longer to recover from, so we now need to build on from here, starting with a plan of action.

GRID-DOWN ACTION PLAN

I'd recommend writing an action plan or a checklist to make sure you cover all the important things if the grid does go down. Of course, this will look a little different for everyone, as your family's requirements and the power you normally rely on will be different, but I can give you a bit of guidance to get you started. I'm just providing you with a checklist at this point, but don't worry: We'll cover all the details throughout the coming chapters.

Day One

- Locate all members of your family, and get everyone home
- Investigate what caused the outage
- Go food shopping
- Fill up water bottles
- Turn the water off at the meter
- Set up your backup power sources
- Deal with frozen and refrigerated food (transfer what you can to coolers)
- Set up the kitchen
- Set up toileting and hand-washing stations
- Set up alternative heating/cooling equipment
- Get the kids to eat up the ice cream!

Next Few Days

- Preserve frozen foods
- Move woodpile to a secure, dry place
- Secure your property
- Disconnect your property from public utilities
- Liaise with the local community

After the First Few Days

- If you have a garden, get to work on food production
- Drain your indoor pipes to prevent freezing (if

necessary)
- Set up a temporary fridge outdoors (i.e., use the shed)
- Get hold of any provisions you're still lacking (e.g., more blankets)

Of course, your list could look quite different to this depending on what you need to take care of in your own home, but I'd definitely recommend having a checklist of some sort. It's easy to panic in an emergency, and a clear plan will keep you focused and make sure you're covering all bases.

Your action plan, however, will be much more effective if you have things in place to see you through a longer-term problem, and that's what we'll start looking at in the next chapter.

TAKE ACTION: CHECKLISTS AND PLANS

At the end of each of the coming chapters, I'm going to give you a practical thing you can do now to help you prepare for the worst. In this case, it makes sense to start with that action plan. So here's your mission: Make yourself a checklist to cover all the essential short-term equipment we've discussed in this chapter, and create your action plan for the first few days of a long-term crisis.

3

A CLOSER LOOK AT OFF-GRID POWER

Before we go any further, let me come clean: I don't live completely off the grid. I still rely on municipal suppliers, but I'm getting closer to a point where I could survive without them if I needed to. And that's becoming increasingly less unusual. A growing number of people are choosing to live off-grid for economic, environmental, and political reasons—and not just preppers. For anyone who wants to be fully prepared for disaster, off-grid options should be a consideration, even if only as additional sources of power. It's always a good idea to have some kind of backup for short-term power outages but if the grid went down completely, having an independent system would mean your family could thrive despite the challenges.

Living off-grid simply means that your home is completely energy-independent. You supply your own power with renewable energy. If you thought growing your own vegetables was satisfying, wait until you try powering a heater with solar energy you've collected yourself! It's important to say at this point that whole books could be written not only on independent energy systems but on each one alone. My aim here is to give you an overview of the options and look at what can be done to prepare a grid-reliant home for a grid-down situation.

A QUICK NOTE ON GOING FULLY OFF-GRID

If you were choosing to live off-grid permanently, you would need to consider your home and your specific needs before deciding on a system. First, you'd need to consider the type of property you live in and its size. To put it simply, the smaller your property, the easier it will be to source enough energy to power it. If you live on a houseboat, or you have a motor home or a bungalow, you could well find that going fully off-grid is a plausible option for you. If you live in a big house, however, you may want to consider downsizing if your aim is to be fully independent.

Where your property is located also makes a difference. Sourcing your own energy is possible in both urban and rural areas, but it's much easier in a rural area because you're more likely to have space for turbines, solar panels, or generators. Also, your neighbors are less likely to complain, and while that might seem like a small point, it's not insignificant.

Lastly, you're going to want to think about regional climate. This will determine the best source of energy for your home. If you live in an area where you get a lot of sunshine, solar power is an obvious choice, while if you get a lot of wind, wind power might be a better idea.

Make sure you consider all these factors if you think a fully off-grid lifestyle might be the direction you want to head in.

OFF-GRID POWER OPTIONS

When it comes to sourcing your own energy, you have a number of options at your disposal. I think it's useful to bear in mind that it's not necessarily a choice you have to make, and you may well find that the best solution for you is to use multiple sources.

Solar Energy

Solar is probably what most people think of when they think of off-grid energy sources, and you can certainly gather a lot of power this way. Boiled down to basics, this involves photovoltaic solar panels and an inverter, which converts the sun's energy into electricity, which is then stored in batteries for later use. The whole system doesn't require much maintenance once you have it set up. However, as yet, it's not particularly cost-effective, and how much power you can produce does depend on your climate. That said, there are now government incentives available in many areas, and you can often sell excess power back to the grid; the chances of it becoming more affordable in the near future are increasing.

Solar panels aren't your only way to harness the sun's energy either. You can make a big difference to your use of energy simply by using specific pieces of solar equipment. You can use solar water heaters, solar cookers, solar lights, solar batteries... Every small change makes a difference.

Wind Energy

It's easy to think of wind power and imagine off-shore wind farms, but it's possible to get much smaller wind turbines for residential use. These are only really an option for powering a whole home if you have a smaller space and live somewhere with high wind speeds. All this said, you do still require significant space to have a wind turbine on your property. The US Department of Energy says in its *Small Wind Guidebook* that a turbine able to generate 5–15 kW of electricity each month would be needed to power the typical home (which uses, on average, 830 kWh a month). To look at an example from the middle of that range, a 10 kW turbine comes mounted on a 100-foot tower, and has a rotor diameter of about 23 feet. You would need to have space to accommodate this safely, and without bothering your neighbors. It's also worth bearing in mind that wind turbines need more maintenance and have more things likely to go wrong with them than solar panels. Wind power also tends to be less reliable: A sudden still day, and you can end up producing no electricity at all. Again, many areas offer government rebates and the option to sell excess power back to the grid, so there are definite plus sides if you can make it work for you.

Geothermal Energy

Geothermal energy is a far less common solution, but it's worth knowing about. The theory behind it is that because the temperature of the Earth (below the frost line) has a constant temperature of 50°F, we can make use of its natural energy to maintain the temperature of our living environment. The way it works is by pumping water to a geothermal unit through underground piping. This then uses the water to cool or heat the air in the home, circulating it around the space through ducts. These systems are usually quite expensive to install, but the amount you save in heating and cooling costs is significant. Of course, the limitation of a geothermal system is that it's only useful for heating and cooling, and while the benefits are substantial, you will need to use other power sources too.

Microhydro Energy

Microhydro energy sounds like it might be a relatively new phenomenon, but watermills are one of the oldest ways to harvest natural energy there is. They rely on turbines catching on moving water, which spins the rotor in order to power a generator. The term "micro" simply comes from doing it on a smaller scale than a traditional watermill. The problem is that unless you live near a river or stream, a water turbine won't work for you. That said, if you do happen to have a stream running through your property, it's a very cost-effective option. Provided that stream doesn't run dry, you can run it every hour of every day, producing a lot of energy for a prolonged period of time. Because it's such a consistent way of producing electricity, you don't need as many batteries for storage. Like wind turbines, however, it's worth bearing in mind that a microhydro system will require a fair amount of maintenance.

Biogas

Biogas is produced when organic matter (think food scraps or animal waste) is broken down in an oxygen-free environment. It can then be used to generate electricity, heat water, or power vehicles. What this means is that if you generate enough food and garden waste, you can use it to produce electricity; all you'll need is a biodigester and a compatible generator. I can't say I've ever used a system like this, but I hear that it's surprisingly easy, although you're unlikely to be able to generate enough power for all your needs. For cooking or heating, though, it could be a good choice for someone with a lot of garden waste.

Generators

So far, we've looked at renewable energy, and from an environmental point of view, this is definitely the way to go. However, even if your aim is to reduce your reliance on fossil fuels, there's a high chance that it'll take you a while to become completely renewable. When you're thinking about ways to add off-grid options to your home for an emergency, the generators commonly used to power log cabins and the like are a good option. And the good news is that some of these rely on renewable energy too. In fact, if you can, I'd say that your best option is to use renewable energy, even for a generator, for the simple reason that if the grid does go down, you're probably going to have a hard time getting hold of diesel or gas.

The first generator we know of was invented by Michael Faraday in 1831. It was a simple device that worked by using a bar magnet to produce an electrical current in a coiled wire. Eventually, this discovery led to the creation of the Faraday disc, which is commonly cited as the first electromagnetic generator. Since those early days, technology has developed significantly, and there are now a number of generator options available to us.

Standby Generators

Standby generators work automatically, but otherwise, they're basically the same as gas generators, which we'll look at in a moment. They have a larger tank (so they're less portable), and can usually provide enough power to see you through 48 hours. What's great about standby generators is that they usually have an automatic transfer function, which means they leap into action as soon as the main electricity supply cuts out. They are, however, very expensive, and they're not affordable to many people. They also require a fair bit of maintenance if you want to make sure they'll catch you in an emergency, which, of course, you do.

Gasoline Generators

Gas generators are the most common types of generator, and they're very user-friendly. They're also relatively cheap and are often portable, which is why they're so commonly used to power log cabins. That said, the more power you want to generate, the bigger the generator will need to be, so for powering your home, a portable model probably isn't your best bet. It's also worth bearing in mind that they're quite noisy, and they produce higher emissions than other types of generators.

Diesel Generators

Diesel generators use a combination of an electric generator and a diesel engine, which requires diesel fuel. They have low maintenance needs and tend to be more energy-efficient than gas generators, without costing much more. They do, however, emit a large amount of harmful gas, and they don't do well in wet conditions. If the grid goes down due to flooding, a diesel generator may not be the helpful companion you were hoping for.

Natural Gas Generators

Natural gas generators use either liquified petroleum or propane to run, and they're very fuel-efficient. They can be stored underground if you wish, which perhaps gives you more options in terms of what else you can use your land for. They have low emission rates, and the fuel is cheaper than fossil fuels. So are the maintenance costs compared to other generators, so this is a good value option. That said, they are expensive to install, and they don't always do well in very cold weather.

Portable Generators

Portable generators usually run on gas or diesel, and they're specifically designed to produce a short-term power supply. Of course, this is the main problem with relying on one as a backup power source: It won't keep you going very long, and you won't be able to power much with it. That said, they're great for a short-term power outage and could be a good addition to a much bigger arsenal. A word of warning though: The emission rates are high, and they shouldn't be used in enclosed spaces.

Solar Generators

As you might expect, solar generators capture the sun's energy and turn it into electricity. They usually have solar panels for harvesting and batteries for storage. Since you'll be using the sun, there are no fuel costs with this type of generator, and you won't need to worry about emissions. The downside is that solar generators are pretty expensive, so the initial outlay is significant. They also require a lot of maintenance, and they tend not to be all that durable.

Inverter Generators

Inverter generators contain an alternator, which produces alternating current (AC) power. This is then converted into direct current (DC) power, which is then inverted back again. They're quiet, and much more fuel-efficient than diesel or gas generators. But perhaps their greatest advantage is that they provide a safe source of power for sensitive devices like phones and tablets. Despite their fuel efficiency, though, inverter generators are quite expensive, and they're costly to install. They also won't be enough to power a large property, and although it doesn't tend to be that expensive, regular maintenance is necessary.

Hydrogen Generators

Hydrogen generators are a comparatively new development, and unlike water turbines, you don't need to live by a stream to run them. They have quite a high power output, and they're easy to run, but they're not as easy to get hold of as we might like, and they're often expensive. They also don't do well in very cold conditions as the water used to fill them can freeze, rendering the whole thing useless, and potentially causing a fault in the generator. It's worth knowing about them, but I'd say they're one to keep an eye on in the future.

Maintaining Your Generator

Every type of generator has a different set of maintenance requirements, but there are a few general guidelines that apply to all models. No matter what type of generator you choose, you'll need to regularly check the cooling system and keep a close eye on the coolant levels. Filters will need an annual clean, and you'll want to check the batteries regularly. Finally, if you don't intend to use your generator on a regular basis, it's important to give it a test run periodically. The last thing you want is to haul your generator out when the grid goes down, only to find that the electrolyte levels in the batteries are wrong.

STORING ELECTRICITY

Generating power isn't the only thing you need to think about; you also need to consider how you're going to store it. If you're using solar, you'll only be generating power during the daylight hours, and if you want to power the lights after dark, you're going to need some electricity stored up. You have 3 main options here: battery storage, heat storage, and inverters (which we discussed in the previous section).

Battery Storage

Whether your power's coming from solar, wind, or water, batteries are a good option for storing renewable energy. The size of battery you need depends on both your energy use and the size of your energy system, but the good news is that any advice you get when investing in a new system will include battery storage recommendations. A well-maintained battery bank can last for at least 5 years, but you will need to replace each battery several times during the course of your system's life.

Heat Storage

There are two variations of heat storage systems: thermal and battery. Thermal storage units are basically heavily insulated water tanks. They can provide hot water and store heat from multiple sources for later use. They generally hold between 54 and 110 gallons, but you can get bigger ones. Heat batteries, meanwhile, store the heat or electricity generated by renewable systems in liquid form, converting them back into a solid as needed. They generally take up less space than a thermal system and don't degrade as easily as standard batteries.

PREPARING AN ON-GRID PROPERTY FOR AN OFF-GRID SITUATION

Of course, the ideal backup system entirely depends on personal preference, your family's energy needs, and details relating to your property and location. However, unless you live in a place that gets little sun, my recommendation for a suburban house currently dependent on the grid is to opt for a backup solar system, or at least to use solar as part of your energy generation system. It's a clean source of power, it's quiet, and you need no additional source of fuel. Maintenance is low, and the uses are diverse. I'd supplement this with a gas or natural gas generator so that you have options when sunlight is in short supply.

Before committing to anything, you're going to want to estimate your energy use. To do that, multiply the power consumption of each appliance by the number of hours you expect to use it. So, for example, a 20 W television, expected to be used for 3 hours, will need 20 x 3 = 60 Wh of power. Once you've estimated the energy needs for each appliance, total the results to give you your total energy consumption figure.

Unless you really know what you're doing, I'd suggest you get a professional in to install and set up a backup solar system, but if you're dead set on doing it yourself, read trustworthy guides, and bear in mind that you need to accommodate solar panels, a charge control, a battery bank, and an inverter. For your gas generator, you will need the generator itself, plenty of fuel (and a way to store it), spare parts in case something goes wrong, and some heavy-duty extension cords.

In our house, we currently have a backup solar system and a propane generator, but I have to say, I'm seriously considering making the move to make us function completely off the grid full time. That said, I'm confident that if you have the right knowledge and backup in place, a regular suburban house connected to the grid could survive a grid-down scenario.

TAKE ACTION: DIY EMERGENCY SOLAR PANEL BATTERY CHARGER

I always like a little DIY action. There's something satisfying about creating a solution you know you can dig out in an emergency. You'll need to have made it (or at least have sourced the materials) before the grid goes down though. The chances of being able to get the supplies you need once disaster strikes are slim.

Here's how you can make your own solar panel backup to charge any 12-volt battery.

What You Need

- 2 x 100-watt solar panels
- 2 x metal hinges
- Self-tapping metal screws

- Wiring harness
- Zip ties
- 20 feet of lead wire
- 4-foot battery leads
- Alligator clips
- Charge controller

The Mission

Step 1

Connect the 2 solar panels with the metal hinges and screws so that they'll fold together, with the wires protected inside and the solar panels exposed.

Step 2

Unite the panels by attaching the wiring harness. Secure all the wires and the harness with zip ties.

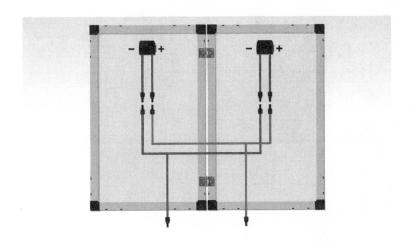

Step 3

Add alligator clips to the ends of the battery leads so you can easily connect your charger to a battery. Keep these leads as short as possible to minimize energy loss.

Step 4

Start with the battery leads. Connect the black lead first to the negative output terminal on your charge controller and then to the negative terminal on your battery. Repeat the process with the red lead and attach it to the positive terminals.

Step 5

Once the battery leads are attached, connect the solar panel lead wires to the charge controller. Once again, start with the negative lead wire.

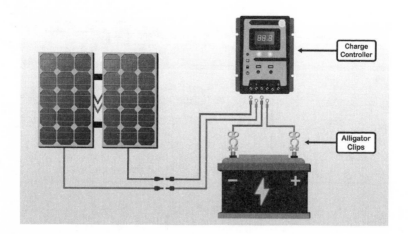

Step 6

Using the manual that came with your charge controller as a guide, adjust the settings to suit the kind of battery you want to charge.

Step 7

To charge, position your solar battery charger in direct sunlight. You may need to reposition the panels throughout the day.

4

LONGER-TERM SOLUTIONS

HEATING AND COOLING

We'll begin this chapter by looking at whole-house systems, but most of the solutions we'll be looking at are for homes that don't have an independent energy system. If you're already self-sufficient in energy (and use a renewable source), you'll be able to power your home if the grid goes down, and your heating and cooling systems will function as usual.

WHOLE-HOUSE SYSTEMS

The majority of you are probably looking for backup solutions, but I think it's worth taking a brief look at whole-house systems so you know what's available in case you're thinking about a bigger overhaul.

Passive Solar Design

Passive solar design simply means using the sun's energy to heat or cool your house through exposure to sunlight. Whenever the sun is shining on your property, the materials it's made of either reflect, absorb, or transmit the radiation. The sun's heat, meanwhile, causes a predictable movement in the air. These facts make it possible for us to design homes that work with the sun to heat and cool themselves. The real beauty of this is that because it works on a design level, it doesn't involve electrical devices or technical components—or at least, it doesn't have to.

There are 5 main elements at work in passive solar design. The first is an aperture, essentially a large window to allow sunlight into the building. To be effective, it should face no further than 30° away from true south, free of shade between 9 a.m. and 3 p.m. The second element is the absorber, an exposed dark surface such as a floor, masonry wall, or water container, which should be in the direct path of the light. This will absorb the sunlight as heat. Below this is the third element, thermal mass, which is made up of materials that will retain the heat. The fourth element is distribution, the means by which solar heat is circulated around the building, transferring through convection, conduction, and radiation. The final element is control, achieved through roof overhangs to shade the aperture during hot spells, electronic sensor devices, vents, and dampers to control heat flow, awnings, and blinds.

Geothermal Heating and Cooling Systems

Much like passive solar design, geothermal heating and cooling systems rely on building design to minimize electricity consumption, using insulation and layout to make the most of the sun's natural heat and the cooling effects of shade. Geothermal systems are often integrated with power from renewable sources, but they're powerful tools in their own right. The earth is a natural thermal insulator, and as we've seen, once you get below the frost line, the temperature remains constant no matter what the weather's doing above ground. Geothermal heating and cooling systems use this to their advantage and draw on this constant temperature to maintain the climate within a building.

A system like this is made up of two key components: a heat pump coming from the ground and a transfer system composed of underground pipes. These pipes contain a solution of water and antifreeze, which will absorb or radiate heat depending on the conditions. This sort of system takes an active approach but you can also take a passive approach to geothermal temperature control... and the chances are, if you have a basement, you're already doing it. The basement of a house will be cooler than the rest of the building during hotter seasons, and this is why they're so useful for storage. Conversely, if your power's out during the winter, you may find that it's the warmest place to be. This is a good tip if you want to see geothermal temperature control in action without redesigning your whole house!

Solar Powered Radiant Heat Floor

Radiant floor heating relies on either tubing heated by water or electric heat coils running under the floor. The heat that rises from the flooring then radiates through the space, warming everything it comes into contact with. This keeps the temperature constant throughout the room, rather than being concentrated in one area. While it may seem like a fairly new approach to temperature control, it's actually very old: The Ancient Romans heated their buildings with under-floor water pipes. Although it does require energy, it's a much more economical approach to heating than a central heating system powered by a furnace, and it can be done off-grid using solar or other renewable sources to provide electricity or heat water.

Biomass Boiler

Much like a traditional gas boiler, a biomass boiler is able to provide a home's heating and hot water. They tend to use wood pellets, but you can use firewood in them, which would be your best option in an emergency situation. If you install a biomass boiler now, you may be able to get some of the cost subsidized by the government (they're included in the incentives program), and since they're reliable and consistent, they make for a good, sustainable way of heating your home. Nonetheless, the upfront costs are considerable, and biomass boilers are quite large, so you'll need to account for the space one will take up. They're fairly labor-intensive, although you can reduce your workload by installing a silo to feed wood into the boiler. Bear in mind that a boiler like this will still need regular maintenance and cleaning.

Solar Chimney

A solar chimney regulates a property's temperature while simultaneously providing ventilation. They're basically hollow containers connecting the inside and outside of the building, and they're an economical way of regulating temperature. The chimney is coated with a black material, which reduces the amount of sunlight reflected back off the chimney, absorbing heat at the same time. In the northern hemisphere, the chimney is usually situated on a south-facing wall in order to get the most sun. Solar radiation hits the chimney, heating the air inside it, and vents at the top of the chimney allow the space to be closed, forcing the warm air back down into the building. As the air cools, the chimney pulls it back in, reheating it inside the enclosure.

Meanwhile, cooling is achieved through vents. While the vent at the top of the chimney can be opened to allow warm air to escape and cooler air to enter, there's also a second vent at the opposite end of the property, which serves as an opening to the outside air, allowing for further ventilation. Although the sun's radiation continues to hit the chimney and be warmed inside it, the chimney vent allows it to escape as cooler air is pulled in.

BACKUP SYSTEMS FOR GRID-RELIANT HOMES

Many of us will continue to rely on the grid for at least some of our energy. Nonetheless, we need to be sure that we can carry our families through tougher times without it. With that in mind, let's take a look at heating and cooling backup plans so that if your supply is cut, you can still keep your family safe and comfortable.

Heating

Preparing Your Home

Even if you're not planning on overhauling your heating system, if you live in a colder region it would be wise to prepare your property for the worst. The bonus of this is that you can reduce your heating costs significantly, even if there's never an emergency to navigate. Start by checking your attic space and adding extra insulation if necessary. Then check your windows and doors: Do they have tight seals? Can you feel a draft coming in around the edges? Are they contributing to the energy efficiency of your home? We recently replaced the windows in our living room, and it's incredible how much difference it has made to the temperature. I'd also suggest thick, heavy curtains, which will not only help you maintain the warmth in the evening when they're shut but will also reduce any draft that is coming in around the window frames.

However, even the most well-insulated house requires extra heat in the winter, and if you find yourself cut off from the grid, it's crucial that you have some backup heating options in place.

Wood Stove

If you have a wood-burning stove, you already have an off-grid backup in place. We have one, and I admit it was originally installed with a power outage in mind but it's actually just a joy to have anyway. If you don't plan to have one permanently, you can install a wood stove on a temporary basis, as long as you have a chimney pipe and a convenient window. Position the stove near to the window, and remove a pane of glass to run the chimney through. You can close the space around the chimney with plywood to keep the warm air in and the cold air out. A word of warning though: If you're planning on installing a temporary wood stove, you're going to want to make sure you get one that uses wood rather than pellets. Many stoves on the market now are fueled by wood pellets, and they're more energy-efficient, but they can't be used with regular firewood. So, as soon as you run out of pellets, your stove is useless. With a regular wood-burning stove, you can source your own firewood no matter what happens to the grid.

Kerosene/Propane Heater

The only real difference between a kerosene and a propane heater is the fuel it burns. Both are an effective way to heat a single room, radiating heat from each side, much like a wood-burning stove. The fuel is loaded into a tank and can be ignited either automatically or manually, depending on the model. Most heaters are portable, which means you can easily move them between rooms, and when there isn't an emergency, they're a great extra heat source to take on a camping trip.

Whether you opt for kerosene or propane is really a matter of choice, although it's worth noting that propane is cheaper and cleaner burning. Many models tend to burn for longer than their kerosene counterparts too. Whichever you choose, though, remember that you'll need to have a good supply of fuel in stock to see you through a crisis. Both can be stored for a fairly long time, but again, propane comes out on top: It will last indefinitely, while kerosene will only last for about 5 years.

I've had a few portable heaters over the years, but the Portable Buddy Heater is my favorite—it has the power to heat up to 225 square feet. You can get 6 hours of low heat out of a 1 pound propane cylinder, or 3 if you want it turned up high.

Gas Catalytic Heater

Arguably, gas catalytic heaters have the upper hand over both kerosene and propane heaters because you don't need to worry about fuel storage, and they don't require a flame to be ignited. They contain a ceramic element, which is filled with natural gas or liquid propane gas, and radiates heat as it burns. If you're wondering how they work, think back to science class: Catalytic combustion occurs when the gas comes into contact with oxygen, producing heat, water, and carbon dioxide.

The great advantage of this type of heater is that you don't need electricity or a stock of natural gas—providing, of course, that you can get to a natural gas pumping station. Of course, should the power be cut for any length of time due to an extreme weather event, it could be that the pipes at the pumping station are damaged, in which case, your heater won't be of much use to you unless you have a stock of liquid propane to use as an alternative. Natural gas does have an indefinite shelf life, but you can't really store it at home because a household tank can't cope with the pressure required to keep it in a liquid state.

Compost Water Heater

If you have a garden, you're going to want to try this. Think of your compost pile and how it steams when you turn it: Compost gets hot while it's decomposing, and you can use that to your advantage. A hose is coiled inside the compost pile, carrying water through it, which is heated by the decomposition process. You might not think that would be enough to generate much heat, but you'd be surprised: Compost can reach up to around 160°F, which is about the same as the average conventional water heater.

You're probably not going to be able to heat a room with this without a significant amount of work, but what you can do is heat water for a hot shower, and that's going to be something you'll be really glad of if you get cut off from the grid. I know, you're dying to try it. I'm one step ahead of you: We'll take a look at how to make one at the end of the chapter.

Urban Igloo

The urban igloo is really just an extension of creating microclimates. It's kind of like the ultimate blanket fort, and you can probably create one without needing anything you don't already have at home. You want to place a mattress beneath a dining table, and then drape thick blankets or rugs over the top so that they hang down the sides to make a tent. You want them to reach the floor, but be careful to leave a gap in one corner so you don't end up with an igloo full of condensation. Just as with a tent or a blanket fort, the more bodies you have inside, the warmer you'll be.

If the igloo experience doesn't appeal to you or you can't face lugging a mattress downstairs, remember you can insulate a room by hanging blankets over doorways. You can get even more from this approach by using a rescue blanket.

Wrapping Up Warm

We discussed clothing in Chapter One, so I won't go over it all again. However, I will remind you that the more you can do to keep your body warm, the less you'll need to worry about heating the room. Remember those layers, cover your head, and make sure everyone has a sleeping bag to snuggle up in during the evening.

Cooling

If you live in a warmer region, or the power supply is cut off during the summer, your concern won't be keeping warm: It'll be keeping cool. There's plenty you can do without the grid to help you here, though.

Preparing Your Home

The best thing you can do in advance is to minimize solar gain on your property, which you can do by increasing the shade covering your house. Planting trees is a long-term game plan, but it's still worth doing if you have the space. Alternatively, you can use awnings to create shade on your walls. Inside, you can use blinds and curtains, or you could consider adding reflective window coatings. You can mimic the effects of a reflective window coating during a crisis by covering the windows with aluminum foil.

Lastly, you want to be able to create a through-draft in your home as far as possible, so look at your current ventilation options and see if you could add further window openings or vents.

Lifestyle Changes

Although there are fewer things you can do to prepare your home in advance than there are for keeping it warm, you can make a few lifestyle changes that will help you out if you find yourself suddenly without power.

During hot weather, it's tempting to keep the windows open permanently, but this is actually a false economy. During the hottest part of the day, all that will happen is that you'll get more heat indoors. Keep them shut during the middle of the day, and open from the evening onward. You also want to make sure you have window shades on every window and shut them during the hottest part of the day. Of course, only you know your property. If a window isn't in the path of direct sunlight at any point during the day, you won't need to shade it.

The next thing you can do is pay attention to keeping your own body cool. My kids discovered one summer that if they spray each other with water and then stand in front of the fan, they can not only have a great water fight, but they can also cool themselves off after running around. I have to hand it to them: It's a great idea, and I've been known to do it myself on a hot day. You can also buy special neckties filled with polymer crystals. You soak them in water and tie them around your neck, and the effect is a soothing coolness throughout your whole body. And, of course, there's your clothing choice. Aim for lightweight fabric, and if you're going to be out in the sun, keep your skin covered, no matter how tempting it might be to rip everything off.

Lastly, think about the amount of heat your household generates throughout the day. If you plan to use a stove or oven, try to do it in the morning before the heat gets up, and while you still have the windows open. Think about cooking methods that generate less heat (slow cookers, for example), or consider cooking outdoors.

Off-Grid Air Conditioning

First of all, unless you live somewhere where the temperature makes air conditioning essential, bear in mind that it uses a lot of power and you may not want to make it a priority. However, I'm aware that in some regions, it can be absolutely unbearable without it, so let's take a look at your options.

A regular air conditioning unit is fairly likely to overload your energy system. They use a ton of energy. You're going to want a much smaller model, such as a mini split unit or a freestanding unit, which you can power using a generator or any other backup power source you're using. What I'd suggest doing is planning its use strategically, particularly if you'll be using batteries that need recharging. Use the morning to charge them, and only when the heat gets unbearable in the afternoon, plug in the air conditioning unit. Once it's cool enough to open the windows again, turn it back off.

Solar Fans

Powered directly by the sun, a solar fan comes with a solar panel, either connected remotely or mounted onto the fan itself. If you connect the panel to a battery pack as well as to the fan, you'll be able to run it even during the night or on overcast days. They are a bit more expensive than regular electric fans, but if you think about how much you'll save in energy costs, it probably evens out over time. Year-round air conditioning isn't necessary where I live, so for me, cooling is really only something I have to think about during the summer, and I have a solar fan. I don't claim to know what's best here, and to an extent, it depends on your needs, but I can tell you that we have a Cowin Solar Fan System, and it does the job nicely. It also has a USB charge port and a built-in LED light, which are good little bonuses.

Your heating and cooling requirements depend entirely on where you live, but they're always going to be important. Keeping warm or cool enough is vital to comfort, but it can also be crucial to survival in more extreme climates. Whatever your household's needs, make sure you've assessed them thoroughly and have the right backup in place before disaster strikes.

TAKE ACTION: DIY COMPOST WATER HEATER

You kind of have to, right?! The good news is, it's very easy, especially if you're already used to making your own compost. You'll need a flexible tube of at least 300 feet (an irrigation pipe will work well), and enough space to accommodate a heap with a 6-foot diameter. You'll also want to stock up on hay, as you'll need to insulate the pile once it's complete.

The trick is to start with a foundation of twigs and sticks before you start adding anything else. Aim to extend this a little further than the edge of the main pile, as this will promote good airflow. In order to accommodate the pipe, you're going to need a fairly big compost pile, and (as with any compost pile) you'll need both nitrogen and carbon to generate heat.

Begin with a 2-inch carbon layer (this is your "brown" waste, so think dry leaves, straw, cardboard, and eggshells). On top of this, add an equal layer of nitrogen (this is your "green" waste, so that's grass clippings, young leaves, and fruit and vegetable waste). Now coil your pipe on top of the upper layer, wet the pile well, and repeat the carbon and nitrogen layering. Press everything down tightly and dampen it again, before coiling the next section of pipe and repeating the whole process. You want to make sure that at least a foot of the pipe extends out from the compost pile. Finish up by insulating it with hay.

After that, it's simply a case of setting up a water source. While the grid's still running, this could be an outdoor faucet, but in an off-grid situation, you'll want to use a water tank. All you need to do then is link it up to a showerhead, and a lovely warm outdoor shower is in your future.

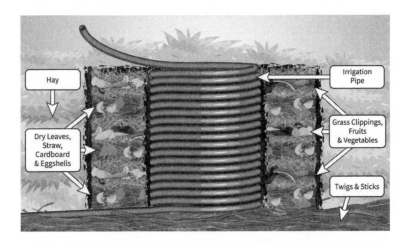

5

LONGER-TERM SOLUTIONS

LIGHTING

I f you have an independent energy system, you'll be able to keep your lights working even if the main grid goes dark. However, if you're totally reliant on the grid or you want to conserve your energy, you'll need backup solutions to see you through a full grid-down scenario. We'll take a look at your options in a moment, but before we do, a quick word on security: If the worst happens, there's a chance that people will become desperate for resources. If your home clearly shows signs that it has precious resources like fuel for lighting, there's a risk that it could become a target for theft. So while I don't want you to panic about this, I do think it's worth mentioning that if you're tempted to light up your house like a Christmas tree, make sure you have blackout blinds up. It's worth doing for heat conservation anyway.

BACKUP LIGHTING SOLUTIONS

Oil Lamps and Lanterns

I mentioned our garden lanterns earlier, but the truth is, they won't necessarily be the best if the grid goes down as a result of extreme weather. Luckily, I do have another lantern: a hurricane lantern. These are designed to stay lit even in strong winds, and although those garden lanterns are a great asset, I'd recommend getting hold of at least one hurricane lantern too.

Mine is a Feuerhand Storm Lantern, and I can't recommend it enough. Its tank holds over half a pint of fuel, and it will burn happily for about 20 hours. It hangs well from a hook or a tree branch, and it can withstand some serious weather. I tried using it with paraffin, which is probably the cheapest kind of fuel you could use for lanterns like this, but quite honestly, I can't stand the smell, so I prefer to use clear lamp oil. It's more expensive, but, for me at least, it's worth it.

If the grid goes down because of an earthquake or a hurricane, however—something which may cause leaks in the gas mains or destabilize the ground—you'd be best off avoiding flammable lighting like this at all. A hurricane lantern is obviously fine for hurricanes, but be mindful of the conditions when you think about lighting lamps.

Oil lamps and lanterns have a distinct advantage when you want to stay warm, in that they also produce heat (and if you want to harness the power of this even further, you can stick some aluminum foil on a wall behind the lamp to reflect the heat back into the room). If you live in a hot climate, however, you might find that some of the other backup solutions will suit you better. You don't necessarily want to be bringing extra heat into the house if you're struggling to keep cool.

If you're considering oil lamps and lanterns, bear in mind that size matters. While a smaller lamp may be useful for carrying around with you, larger models will have wider wicks, and will therefore produce more light. Personally, I'd focus on larger lamps, and keep your flashlight for carrying around with you. It's safer anyway. You'll also need to make sure you stock up on fuel and all the relevant wicks. Most lamps will take paraffin, clear lamp oil, or kerosene, and you can also burn citronella, which has the added bonus of keeping insects away in the summer.

Bear in mind that whether they contain candles or oil, lamps and lanterns are fire risks, so make sure you keep them away from clothing, soft furnishings, and other flammable items. I'd also recommend keeping a fire extinguisher in your house. Hopefully, you'll never need it, but why take the risk?

Propane Lanterns

Propane lanterns are also a good consideration. They run on one-pound propane cylinders, and much like oil lamps, they also generate heat. They will need to be kept away from flammable items, and should only be used in well-ventilated areas. There is some risk of carbon monoxide poisoning, so make sure you have a carbon monoxide detector in your home. You'll need to make sure you have a good stock of propane too. Remember that propane lasts indefinitely, so there's no reason not to keep a good amount in stock.

Candles

Some garden lanterns are designed for candles, and of course, you can also light your living area with naked candles in an emergency. I wouldn't want to rely on them, but I definitely think anyone who wants to be prepared should have some in stock for emergencies. Apart from anything else, they're going to be your best bet if we find ourselves in a grid-down situation due to EMP because of their lack of electrical components.

Look for thick candles like church candles, or candles set in jars. These burn for longer and are less likely to fall over. Your best bet, however, is an emergency candle like the SDS Liquid Oil Candle. It's not a traditional candle, in that it burns liquid paraffin instead of solid wax, but it's still sold as a candle, and it has a burn time of around 115 hours, which is far more than a traditional candle. If you're looking at traditional solid candles, look for emergency options with a burn time of at least 36 hours, but bear in mind that most of these can't be reused.

With traditional candles, the fact that they can be reused is a definite bonus, despite their shorter burn time. If you keep fresh wicks in stock, you can melt down the leftover wax to make new candles. Keep jars on hand to keep them in: The more you can protect the flame, the safer your family will be. Again, though, a fire extinguisher wouldn't be a bad idea.

LED Lanterns

Moving away from the more old-school options but sticking with the lantern theme, LED lanterns are a good option. These can light whole rooms, and they're pretty energy efficient, with a good run time. If you live in a hotter region, this will be a better option for you than an oil or propane lantern, as they run cooler than their traditional counterparts. The other advantage they have is that they don't come with the same fire risk, and you don't have to worry about storing oil or propane. That said, you will need a stock of batteries, or a way of recharging rechargeable models (although some lanterns come with built-in solar panels to sidestep this issue).

I have a Streamlight Siege X in my bug out bag, which is quite small compared to a lot of lanterns. It's a great little lantern for a portable kit, but if you're looking for something for the home, you might prefer a bigger model.

Solar Lights

Solar lights are a great option for outdoor lighting, and they've come a long way in recent years. We have a set lining the path up to our front door, and they really do make a difference in the evening. They don't produce loads of light but they're good for illuminating walkways. If you opt for motion-activated ones (for instance, mounted on your garage), this also provides you with a bit of a security boost, even if the grid is down.

You can use solar lights indoors as well, of course, and in an emergency situation, they might be a good option for placing in hallways and on the stairs—areas where you need to be able to see where you're going but don't need light for anything more. Pro tip: Leave them out in the sun during the day, and in the evening, bring them indoors and push the spikes into Styrofoam blocks to keep them the right way up. Then you can put them wherever you like.

Battery-Operated Lighting

The most obvious type of battery-operated lighting is the flashlight, but you have a few other options at your disposal too. You can get stick-on lights, which are useful if you want something you can easily move about, and again, these are a good option for hallways and the like. They don't tend to give off a lot of light, but they have a soft glow so they're good for areas in which you don't need bright lighting. They usually have a Velcro attachment, allowing you to fit them just about anywhere. Remember to check what batteries they need and add a good amount to your stockpile.

I wouldn't want to rely solely on battery-operated lights, simply because at some point, you're going to run out of batteries. I'd prioritize things you can recharge or stock a good amount of fuel for. That said, flashlights and head-lamps are an absolute must, in my opinion. Refer back to Chapter Two for my advice on these.

What we didn't talk about earlier, however, was the everyday carry (EDC) flashlight. I'd really recommend everyone in the family has one of these in their pocket or handbag. It will mean you'll all have something with you the moment the power goes out. You could opt for much better models, but on the grounds that I wanted to make sure we all had something for the immediate problem, I've opted for a more budget-friendly route for my family. We have Maglite XL50s, which are strong and reliable, despite not being as bright as other models. You'll need to stock some AAA batteries for these.

Chemical Light Sticks

You're most likely to see a glow stick at a festival these days, but they're not a bad idea to keep on hand for an emergency, and like solar lights, they can be good in those high-traffic areas like hallways. I think maybe my favorite thing about them, though, is that they'll make the whole experience a bit more fun and a bit less scary for the kids.

Some of them will actually carry on glowing for about 12 hours. They might not be the most environmentally-friendly option, but they're fun; reliable for a short time; and a handy, easy-to-store extra to have on hand.

Lighting is always important, particularly on shorter days. The good news is that all these solutions are simple and easy to stock up on in advance. I'd recommend having a number of different options available to see you through both a short-term and longer-term crisis. This way, no matter what the catalyst for the grid going down is, you'll know you have lighting options that will work.

TAKE ACTION: DIY EMERGENCY LIGHT

Regardless of all the lighting options there are out there, I can't resist a good DIY light, and if it involves food, all the better! Any well-stocked pantry should have a supply of oily fish, and if yours includes tinned sardines, there's a bonus lighting project you can embark on.

This will only work with sardines packed in oil, but once you've enjoyed your sandwich, keep the oil and the tin, and make your own fishy oil lamp (yes, it does smell a little, I'll be honest). Simply add a natural fiber wick to the oil in the tin. Once it's completely soaked, light the end, and you'll be surprised by how long that little lamp will burn.

If you'd prefer a tastier-smelling project, collect your excess bacon fat in a jar until you have enough to turn into a candle. Simply coat a natural fiber wick in fat, push it right down to the bottom of the jar, and voila: a delicious-smelling DIY candle. Word of warning though: I've tried this, and it drives the family crazy if you're not also going to offer them a bacon sandwich!

6

LONGER-TERM SOLUTIONS

WATER FILTRATION AND STORAGE

I'm lucky enough to have never been in a situation where I haven't had access to water, but during our recent power outage, I realized that in the event of a serious grid-down emergency, it wouldn't just be the electricity and gas we'd lose: It would be water too. So I've reassessed my stockpiles and started thinking more seriously about what we'd do if we lost access to running water.

WHY WATER IS A PRIORITY IF THE GRID GOES DOWN

If millions of people are affected by a large-scale power outage, it won't be long before the water supply is affected. We don't think about it much, but the running water in our homes is made possible by timers, valves, pumps, and substations, and when they're no longer able to provide enough water pressure to keep the water flowing, it's all going to stop. We can only live about 3 days without water, so making sure you have it is going to be a top priority in a grid-down situation.

The first thing to remember is that you need more water than you probably think you do. Drinking water is clearly a priority but you'll also need water to meet your family's hygiene needs, for washing dishes, for doing laundry, and for cooking. We looked at your short-term water needs earlier in the book, but if we're looking at a longer-term crisis, you're going to need between 20 and 30 gallons of water for every member of the household per month. I'm of the point of view that it's always best to err on the side of caution, so I'd estimate your needs nearer the higher end of the spectrum. That means a family of 4 would need about 360 gallons of water to see them through 3 months... and for that reason, you'll need to think carefully about storage. But don't worry: We'll get to that shortly.

WHAT YOU CAN DO IN ADVANCE OF A CRISIS

Just as you can make your home crisis-ready in terms of heating or cooling, you can prepare for an event that leaves you without water.

If you're a gardener, you probably already harvest your own water. If you're not, you should know that having a garden isn't the only reason you might want to consider doing so. If the water you collect is to be fit for human consumption, it will need to be purified (which we'll look at further down the chapter), but there are some household tasks (flushing the toilet, for example) for which this isn't necessary.

To collect rainwater, you need 5 basic elements: a catchment surface (like your roof); a way to direct the rainwater to your collection system (the gutters and downspouts on your property); a filter to keep debris out of the water; a lidded barrel to collect it; and a faucet to release it from the barrel. This should be installed low on the barrel, and ideally, you want to include a way of directing overflow (a lot of people use a hose connected to a backup barrel for this). The good news is that as you want to install this well in advance of an emergency, you can get a complete system from your garden or hardware store.

The other thing you can do well in advance is stock up on bottled water. This will only last you for a short time, but I would aim to store enough to keep your family going for the first couple of weeks of a disaster. It will keep indefinitely if you store it in a cool dry place. Keep it out of direct sunlight, and aim not to store it in contact with a cement floor or wall (this can transfer chemicals into the water). To avoid leakage, avoid stacking water containers too high, and rotate your stock to make sure it's all in good condition (single-use plastic deteriorates over time). Tempting as it may be to fill old containers with tap water, remember that juice, milk, soda, and water bottles aren't designed to be reused. Most of them contain polyethylene terephthalate (PET), and they can leach chemicals into the water if they're reused.

WATER STORAGE OPTIONS

Beyond your initial supply of bottled water, you're going to need to think about how you're going to store water for a longer period in such a way that you can replenish it as necessary. Before we get to my recommendations for this, a word of caution: Avoid gallon jugs. They're comparatively cheap, but you'll quickly find that they're a hindrance to your whole storage system because you can't stack them. They can also be quite flimsy, and all it takes is for one to be caught on something, and you have water all over the floor and one less gallon in your stash. There are other options that are much more reliable and easy to store.

Portable Water Storage Containers

A better alternative is portable water containers, which typically hold between 5 and 7 gallons of water. You can get larger ones, but the heavier they are, the less portable they become, and the harder it will be to take water from them. A good option is the Reliance Aquatainer. With a 7 gallon capacity, it's sturdy, easy to store, and has a spigot for easy use. It also has a liquid level indicator, which is a useful bonus. I've seen these in Walmart, and they're not all that expensive, so they're easy to get hold of and stock up on in advance. For me, the spigot really is a game-changer. We use these when we go camping, and it works a bit like a wine box: You can just leave it on a camping table and use it as necessary. There's no wastage, and even the clumsiest child can use it independently.

I would aim to store enough water to see your family through two months in containers like these. The added advantage of using them, even if you also have a tank or a barrel, is that you can easily take them with you if you need to evacuate your home.

When you're using containers like this, you're going to want to refill them every six months or so, discarding the old water and rinsing them well. Without doing this, you run the risk of bacteria breeding in your water, and that's the last thing you want in an emergency situation.

Storage Barrels and Tanks

It does require you to have a bit more space, but if you have the luxury, a water tank or barrel is a good idea. I can't say they're cheap, but they do allow you to store a large amount of water for a considerable amount of time. They come in a range of sizes, so if you have a garage or a basement, you should be able to clear a big enough corner for one. You can store between 50 and 250 gallons of water this way.

For the average suburban family, a water cistern is an unrealistic option, but it's worth mentioning anyway. These tanks will hold several thousand gallons of water and are usually buried beneath the ground. Many people link them up to their rainwater harvesting system. If you do consider this route, however, it's important to make sure you choose a cistern made of food-grade materials and don't buy one that has previously been used for chemical storage.

Cistern, barrel, or tank, you'll have to take an extra precaution with storing water in this volume: You'll need to treat it in order to prevent bacterial growth. You can buy water treatment drops (Water Preserver is a trustworthy brand)—just follow the instructions on the bottle. We'll also look at some other purification methods further down the chapter.

Aqua Pods and WaterBOBs

You could also consider something like an Aqua Pod or a WaterBOB, which are essentially plastic bladders you put in the bath and fill from the faucet. As they fill with water, they mold to the shape of the bathtub, keeping your water supply safe and secure. Of course, you could just put the plug in and fill the bath before the water cuts out, and if you don't have a device like this, it's still worth doing. But the advantage of these products is that they'll protect your supply from bacteria and any unpleasant extras that might be lingering in the bathtub. A WaterBOB will hold 100 gallons of water and keep it fresh for around 16 weeks; an Aqua Pod will take 65 gallons, keeping it fresh for about 8 weeks.

Containers like this are designed for single-use, so once you've used your supply, you can't use them again. That said, you probably wouldn't need to: They're designed to be filled from the faucet, and once that's no longer an option, you won't have any use for it again. Don't be tempted to keep them to reuse in the future though: Bacteria will grow inside them, and they won't be safe.

Personally, I'd recommend having something like this so you can make the most of your bathroom faucet as soon as you realize there's a problem. It's an easy way to top up your supply straight away, and it's more hygienic than filling the bathtub without any kind of protective container.

IF THE GRID GOES DOWN: WHAT TO DO IMMEDIATELY

When the grid goes down, the water supply hasn't got long. The first thing to do is to collect as much water from the faucets as you can. If you have a WaterBOB or an Aqua Pod, now's the time to fill it. If you don't, put the plug in the bath, and fill it anyway. Put buckets at the bottom of your gutter downspouts to collect any extra rainwater that might come your way, and lay a piece of tarpaulin outside to collect groundwater (you can angle this so it drains into a bucket too). Fill any empty storage containers from the sink faucets, and fill bowls and buckets too. The water you collect in these won't keep for as long, but you can use it for your immediate needs. The mission at this stage is simply to collect as much water as possible before the system runs dry.

THE WATER YOU SHOULD NEVER DRINK

Once you've been living without power for a while and you're beginning to go through your water stocks, you're going to have to think about sourcing more water. However, before we get to that, it's important to bear in mind that not all water is safe for drinking. Some of these things may seem obvious, but if you're panicking, it's easy to forget the basics, so I don't think it's wise for me to assume that anything's too obvious to mention.

Avoid water from the toilet cistern and bowl, the radiators, your pool, or any water beds you may have. All of this water could be contaminated, and shouldn't be used without treatment. You should also avoid drinking flood-water or water from a well unless it has been declared safe. This is worth noting because in the event of a natural disaster, well water that may previously have been deemed safe could be contaminated. Don't trust it unless it has been tested and given the all-clear. Finally, if you live near the ocean, don't be tempted to drink the salt-water without distilling it first.

SOURCING WATER FROM THE WILD

I say "wild," but there's water hiding from you all over the place, not just in natural bodies of water.

Your first source is, of course, rainwater, and if you've installed a water barrel, you'll already have been collecting it before disaster strikes. It can contain contaminants, however, so you'll need to filter and purify it. If you don't have a rainwater harvesting system, you can still collect rainwater in buckets.

Your hot water tank is also a source of emergency water and probably contains around 30 gallons. To drain the water, you'll need to turn off the supply and the power (even if neither of these things is working). If yours is a gas heater, switch the thermostat to the Pilot setting. The drain valve will be near the bottom of the heater. Connect this to a garden hose, and then turn on a hot water faucet nearby. Put the other end of the hose into a bucket before opening the valve. I'd recommend gathering several buckets before you start because you'll definitely need more than one. That said, you don't necessarily need to drain the whole tank at once—you can always close off the valve and drain the rest later. You may notice some mineral deposits once you get to the end of the water, but these aren't harmful and you can easily filter them out.

The next place to look for water is in your neighborhood. Streams, ponds, rivers, lakes... All of this depends on where you live, of course, but unless you live in the desert, you're likely to have some water nearby. This is where those water storage containers will really come into their own but bear in mind that you'll need to be able to carry whatever you collect. If you have a handcart or a wheelbarrow, this might be a good way of being able to carry several containers further.

Treating Water

Any water you do collect will need to be treated before it's safe to drink. Your first option is filtering. I use a Big Berkey Water Filter, mostly because of its shelf life: Each element will filter around 3,000 gallons. We often take it camping with us because it's powerful enough to purify stream water, and it's made of steel, so it's easy to transport without damaging it. There are plenty of other brands out there though, so you have options. Just make sure you have a supply of filters on hand. Whichever system you use, strain the larger debris away before you run the water through it in order to keep your filter clean and running for longer.

You can mimic the effects of a water filter by using natural filters. If you add a layer of sand to the bottom of a straining container, followed by layers of charcoal and rocks, you can run your water through it to minimize the bacteria levels. Bear in mind, however, that this will not get rid of giardia if it is present.

Alternatively, you could boil your water, which will kill any bacteria lurking inside it. Simply bring it to the boil and allow it to continue for 10 minutes or so, before leaving it to cool. It won't be the tastiest water you've ever drunk, but it will be safe... and you can always make tea with it to enhance the flavor.

You can also get UV pens designed to kill water-borne bacteria. Again, you'll want to strain any debris off first. I can't vouch for these as I've never tried one personally, but I do know people who've used them on camping trips and say they work well.

Chlorine bleach is another alternative, but you need to be careful. It's technically carcinogenic and can lead to poisoning, but if you're out of other options, it can be a useful last resort. Avoid scented bleach or bleach with added chemicals, and double-check the expiry date first (you might be surprised to know that it's only effective for 6 months). Don't use pool chlorine: It's much stronger than domestic bleach, and this is why you shouldn't drink the water in your pool. You'll need just 8 drops of bleach for every gallon of water, but again, strain off any debris first. Shake your container well, and leave it for 30 minutes before using it.

I hold my hands up and admit that I'm a little nervous of using chlorine bleach myself. I'd do it if I had no other option, but if I was going to use chlorination, I'd prefer to use chlorine dioxide tablets. They kill many different viruses and bacteria (including giardia, which chlorine bleach won't), and they're easy to use: All you need to do is add the tablets to the water—just follow the instructions on the packet. You can also get the same thing in liquid form, the only difference being that you add drops rather than tablets.

Alternatively, you could opt for distillation. This requires a bit more planning and equipment, but if you want to follow that route, you can always set yourself up in advance. To distill water, you require a heat source, a heat-resistant container, a condenser, and another container to collect the distilled water. You'll also need a tube (made of food-grade materials) to transport the steam from the first container, through the condenser, and into the second container. You can actually buy countertop distillers for around $200, which might be your best bet if you're willing to make the investment.

CONSERVING WATER

No matter how good your storage and collection plan is, you want to be mindful of how much water you're using, and conserve what you can. This doesn't mean drinking less than you need, but you can be mindful of what you eat in order to reduce unnecessary thirst. Try to avoid salty foods if water is becoming scarce, as these will make you more thirsty. Bear in mind that the human body does need sodium though, so don't go overboard; just rein in your potato chip obsession. We'll look at laundry and dishwashing specifically a little later, but this is definitely an area in which you can conserve water. Wait until you have a good load before you contemplate using precious water for it. You could even opt for disposable cups and plates to minimize the number of dishes that need washing.

If there's one thing I want you to take away from this chapter, it's this: It would be wise to calculate how much water you're going to need to get your family through at least a month without water, ideally 3 months. It will probably be more than you expect, so make those calculations now—and don't forget to account for your pets.

TAKE ACTION: CALCULATE YOUR FAMILY'S WATER NEEDS

Remember the golden rule: 1 gallon per person per day. So, to calculate your family's water needs, you can use the following equation:

Water requirements = (1 gallon) x (number of people) x (number of days)

This will give you your family's drinking and sanitation requirements, but you'll also need to add on water for cooking and pets. As a guideline, most dogs need about 1 ounce of water per pound of body weight every day. You'll also need to account for your regional climate: If you live somewhere hotter, you're going to need more water.

7

LONGER-TERM SOLUTIONS

FOOD AND COOKING

The best advice I can give you when it comes to cooking when the power's out is to practice. Being prepared means being prepared with your skills and knowledge as much as it does with your supplies. So when I say the best thing you can do is practice, what I mean is, you need to practice alternative cooking methods *before* disaster strikes. At least, you do if you want to avoid culinary disasters, and let me tell you, I've learned this the hard way. Just ask my kids about the first time I tried to roast a shoulder of lamb on the campfire...

It would be best to prepare to cook both indoors and outdoors. Cooking outside is safer for some methods, and if you live in a warm region, you're going to want to keep the extra heat inside to a minimum. But it may be that the weather is too bad for you to cook outdoors, which means you need to be prepared to cook inside too. Of course, you won't necessarily need to practice every method of cooking there is, but it would be wise to have skills to cover a few approaches.

OFF-GRID COOKING OPTIONS

The first thing I would say is that the best cooking method depends entirely on what it is you're cooking, and that's why it's a good idea to be familiar with a few approaches. It will also mean you'll need to have a few different types of fuel on hand to use with whichever devices you'll be cooking on, so bear this in mind when you're taking an inventory of your supplies.

Camping Stove

There are two main routes you can go down with camping stoves: gas stoves and alcohol stoves. Gas stoves are typically fueled by canisters of propane, butane, or isobutene, and a few models allow you multiple options. If you only have a small stove for camping, it might be worth getting something that connects to a larger cylinder for long-term disaster preparedness. Word of warning though: Not all camping stoves are certified for indoor use, and you'll always need to ensure that you have good ventilation, even with those that are. We have a butane stove that has been certified for use indoors, and I've tested it out at home as well as for camping. It fits neatly on the kitchen counter, and it almost feels like cooking on a regular stove. What I would say, though, is that butane cylinders aren't cheap, and these stoves burn through a lot, particularly if you'll be doing long, slow cooking. They'd be great for a short-term outage, but you'll want something else up your sleeve to cover a longer crisis.

The other type of camping stove is an alcohol stove, which typically burns alcohol, pure methanol alcohol, or pure ethanol. A lot of people seem to prefer alcohol stoves to gas stoves, but you definitely want to get your practice in. It takes a bit of perseverance to get the hang of heat control, and I can't say I've mastered it myself.

There is an alternative route with camping stoves too: portable wood stoves, which actually require very little wood. I've never used one (I'm a big fan of a campfire), but I have friends who swear by them. They work by trapping the heat so you can cook with little fuel, and have a built-in pot stand. They're sort of a halfway house between camping stoves and wood stoves.

Wood Stove

If you're heating your home with a wood stove anyway, you have the added option of using it for cooking. Bear in mind that all wood stoves should be properly installed with adequate ventilation—this isn't just something you can add on a whim for cooking purposes.

If you do decide to cook on your wood stove, you can basically cook anything you would usually cook on your regular stove, but you'll need to come to grips with controlling the heat. This is simply a case of getting to know your stove. Start by finding out where it gets hottest: This will be where you can cook food quickly. As you move further away from this "sweet spot," your food will cook at a slower rate. You can also control the temperature by adjusting how you build the fire. If you opt for several thinner logs in place of one large one, they'll burn more quickly and generate more heat.

Campfire

A wood stove is your indoor fire option. If you don't have one or you'd prefer to cook outside, a campfire is totally an option, as long as the weather is onside and you have suitable space for a firepit. As you'll know if you've ever tried to embrace your inner caveman on a camping trip, however, campfire cooking is a skill. I've burned many a pan of beans over an open fire, let me tell you.

Before you build your firepit, you want to check the wind direction to make sure that the smoke won't be blowing toward where you're planning to eat. With this established and a good spot chosen, you'll need to dig a pit and mark a perimeter around it with stones. Dig further down in the center, which will make the fire less likely to escape.

Your next step is choosing firewood. I would recommend stocking up on kindling in advance because it saves you searching for dry twigs, which can be tricky in damp conditions. Otherwise, this is the first thing you'll need to do, as well as searching for larger pieces of wood. Look for broken branches and deadwood. If you cut branches directly from trees, they'll contain too much moisture to burn well. If you have a choice, go for hardwoods like ash, oak, or birch, rather than softwoods like spruce or pine. Softwoods get going quickly, but they don't burn for as long and don't allow you as much control when you're cooking.

You then want to lay your firewood, and there are several ways you can approach this. Personally, I'm a fan of the tepee style, which works with a tepee-like structure to allow air circulation and concentrate the flame. I've always found this method to be reliable, and it's easy to construct. Start by sticking a forked branch into the ground as a center pole, and then stack your wood up against it to form a tepee shape. Remember to leave a gap for adding and lighting the kindling.

Once you have your fire burning, you want to let it blaze for a little while before you start cooking. As it burns, it will produce embers, and it's these (rather than flames) that you'll need to cook over. Spread the embers out, being careful not to poke them so much they die out, and let the fire keep burning. Your goal is to have a bed of embers and a roaring fire from which you can keep topping it up.

We'll look more closely at the cooking equipment you'll need further down the chapter, but it's worth mentioning that you'll want a grilling rack to place over the embers. You can also wrap your food in foil and place the packages directly in the embers to cook. Again, this is something you want to practice before disaster strikes because it can take some trial and error to get it right.

Reflector Oven

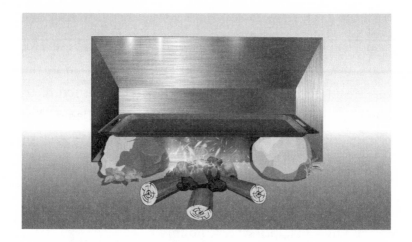

You can take your campfire cooking a step further by building a reflector oven. You'll just need a piece of sheet metal and a cookie sheet or grill pan to put inside. Fold the sheet metal in half to make the main body, and then cut two right-angled triangles to make the sides, along with some tabs to interlock the pieces. I'd recommend using proper metal tools for this, but you can just use some garden snips if you're careful. Then it's simply a case of putting it together and integrating it into your campfire, placing it beside the glowing embers. You'll probably need to place some stones behind it to make it stand up properly. The idea is that it uses radiant energy from the fire to cook the food inside it, so you'll need to keep drawing embers from the fire to keep it at a constant temperature. You can actually bake cakes and pies like this, but you'll definitely need to practice.

Earth Oven

Alternatively, you could set up your backyard for outdoor cooking with an earth oven. This is relatively easy to construct yourself with a little elbow grease, but you'll want to do it well in advance of any disaster so you know you have it as an option as soon as you need it. You'll also want to get hold of some masonry sand for best results. Start by preparing a base: You can either build directly onto the ground, or you can build it up to a more convenient height by using logs, rocks, or concrete blocks.

Aim for a floor size of between 20 and 30 inches, and create it by laying bricks on a level bed of sand about 6 inches deep. Make sure any bricks you use are free from old mortar and make sure they're pressed into the sand firmly to create a surface as flat as possible. What you want to do next is pile moist sand on top of the bricks and flatten it down, creating a dome shape between 16 and 20 inches high. You'll need a bit of math next: Measure the sand form and multiply its height by 0.63 to work out the height of your oven door.

You then want to find some good mud from beneath the topsoil in your backyard. This should contain clay, which will hold your oven together. It should feel a bit greasy and be sticky to the touch. If you're unable to find this in your backyard, you can always collect some from a riverbank or a construction site. Mix 1 part clay soil into 3 parts masonry sand, and add water until a cement-like consistency is reached (this will take some muscle!). Before you go further, you want to test the strength of your mixture by making a tight ball and dropping it from a height. If it cracks, you want to add more water. Once you have a strong, firm mixture, you can start building your oven.

Cover the sand dome with smooth, wet newspaper to stop the walls from sticking. Now add a 3-inch layer of mud, and pack it solidly against the sand base. You might find it helpful to use a board for this. Allow this layer to dry before adding another layer. You could even cover this with plaster for an extra finish once the final layer has dried. Bear in mind that this is a slow process: Drying could take up to a week. Once the mud can be touched without denting, it has dried sufficiently.

Once the outside of the oven is built and dried, you can remove the sand dome, but before you do that, make a mark in the mud where the doorway should be (use the measurement you took earlier). Remove the sand, and smooth out the doorway with a spoon or a stone.

To make the door, cut out a template that will fit the opening, and use this to craft a door out of the clay mixture. It doesn't need to fit perfectly because you can always cover it with a damp towel, which will help with the cooking process and prevent the door from charring.

If you've got this far, it's worth the extra effort to make a covering for your oven. In wet weather, it will become damp, and this can extend cooking time significantly. Just be sure to leave enough room around the oven to allow good air circulation: Think roof rather than snug covering.

Finally, your oven is ready to use. Build a fire inside, allowing smoke to escape through the doorway. Fire it for around 3 hours (or until the black soot at the top has disappeared), and then pull out the coals. Put your food inside, and close the door. This is a great little garden project anyway, I think, disaster or no disaster. Once you've got your practice in, you'll be well equipped to make pizza and bread al fresco any time you like.

Thermal Oven

This seems like a logical point to turn our attention toward alternative ovens. We'll start with the hay box or thermal oven, which is essentially a box that traps heat for long, slow cooking. It's not one to use for a quick evening meal, but if you plan in advance, it provides a good opportunity for conserving fuel. It's also one of the very few cooking options that you don't have to monitor the whole time, and it's a great method for cooking stews or other meals that need to be simmered for a good chunk of time. It's pretty easy to make a DIY thermal oven. You'll need an insulated box such as an old cooler, or a shoebox lined with aluminum foil or old clothing. A lidded saucepan or casserole dish is then placed inside the oven, and the box (if you take the traditional hay box approach) is surrounded with hay for further insulation. You could even make your own box out of wood and insulate it with polystyrene and cardboard if you're skilled in this area. A well-made thermal oven like this won't require the extra hay.

To cook with a thermal oven, you'll need to start your food off over another heat source. Let's say you were making a stew: You would cook all your ingredients as usual, and bring your meal to the boil. You would then remove it from the heat and put it into your thermal oven, where it would continue cooking without additional fuel for a further 8–12 hours. I've tried making stews this way, and I have to say, the results can be quite mind-blowing.

You can also buy commercial thermal cookers. The Wonder Oven is a popular choice.

Tealight Oven

I like to talk about the "tealight oven" as opposed to the Home Emergency Radiant Cooking (HERC) oven because it sounds so much more relatable, but they're the same thing. I was astounded the first time I came across these. If you've ever used a tealight in a candle holder, you'll know that they don't give off a lot of heat on their own. However, if you shelter them in an enclosed space, that space will trap heat and create an oven effect. It's another slow one though, and you'll need several hours to cook an ordinary oven recipe in one, but it's a good alternative to be aware of.

You can buy a specially designed HERC oven, or you can make your own using tealights. To reach a high enough temperature for cooking, you'll need about 12 tealights. Remove the elements and plug from an old toaster oven, and drill some holes in the back. Line the bottom of the oven with tealights, and if you can, attach a piece of baking stone to the top. It should still work fine without this, but you stand a better chance of your food cooking evenly with the stone in place. Because there are flames involved, you'll want to cook on the upper rack rather than the lower one, or you run the risk of your food burning.

Solar Cooking

An alternative outdoor oven option is a solar oven, which you could buy or you could make DIY-style. What's great about this is that you don't need to use up any of your fuel stocks, but it's most effective when the UV Index is above 7. It's a relatively slow cooking method, but it allows the food to retain its moisture, so it offers good results. One brand I hear recommended time and time again is Global Sun Ovens, so if you're thinking of buying one, check them out. If you can afford it, buying one is probably a good idea simply because of the size and stability offered by a professionally built one. However, you can make a small-scale version with a clean pizza box if you're interested in exploring.

Start by drawing a square within 1 inch of the edges of the box lid. Cut out 3 sides of this square with a knife, and crease the uncut side to make a flap. Next, cut out a piece of aluminum foil to cover the internal side of the flap, pressing it down tightly and securing it with tape. Now line the bottom of the box with black paper. Cut 2 squares of plastic wrap the same size as the top part of the box, and secure this to the inside edges of the window. You want this to be airtight. Stuff the sides of the box with rolled-up newspaper as insulation, making sure that the lid will still close.

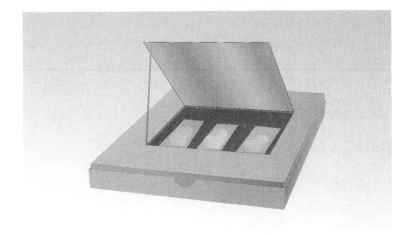

You won't be able to cook a lot with a DIY oven like this, but it'll do in a pinch, and it's a fun project to do with the kids. It'll work best when the sun is at its highest, so between 11 a.m. and 2 p.m. is your best bet. Simply put a dish inside, angle the reflective flap toward the sun, and you're good to go. The black paper inside the oven will absorb energy from the sun, and the warm air will stay inside because of the plastic wrap.

Portable Solar Power Stations

With the exception of wood stoves and camping stoves, most of your alternative cooking methods limit you to cooking outdoors, but there is one more option for indoor cooking. You could use a portable power station (or use your generator, if you have one) to run your stove. However, these can be quite pricey, and you'll need to make sure that they're designed to power energy-guzzling appliances like electric stoves before you buy one. The advantage of a portable solar power station over a generator is that you can charge them outdoors in the sun and then bring them in fully charged. Of course, opting for something like this gives you plenty of other options besides cooking too.

Barbecue Grill

I don't want to explain your barbecue grill to you here, but I do want to bring it up because barbecuing is an excellent option (weather conditions permitting) in a power outage. Plus, it's likely to be something you've already had a lot of practice with. Just make sure you have a good supply of charcoal, and you'll be able to cook outdoors without the use of any more complicated equipment.

I've chosen what I think are the most realistic cooking options to discuss here, but search around online, and you'll find dozens of alternative cooking methods. If you feel like going further down the rabbit hole, check out hobo stoves, wick stoves, and buddy burners. At the very least, there's a lot of educational fun to be had with the family discussing cooking methods and trying out DIY projects.

OFF-GRID COOKING ESSENTIALS

I often speak to people who think they're fully prepared in the cooking department, confident in their knowledge that they have some solid alternatives to grid-reliant cooking up their sleeves. But, what many people don't realize is that alternative cooking methods require alternative equipment. If you're cooking over an open fire, your cheap non-stick frying pan is quickly going to become useless.

First off, let's look at what you definitely want to know you have at home, starting with aluminum foil. Foil has played a role in a few of the DIY projects we've mentioned but it's also a really good resource. As well as keeping food fresher for longer, you can use it for open-fire cooking and for making emergency containers if necessary. It may seem obvious, but the next thing you definitely want to have is a good can opener... possibly two in case anything goes wrong with your first one. You should have a lot of cans in your pantry: Make sure you can get into them! You'll want a bottle opener, pot holders and oven mitts, and wooden spoons. It might seem strange to draw attention to wooden spoons, but if you're used to cooking with plastic utensils, you may find yourself in melted plastic hell if you don't have a backup option for some of these cooking methods. Lastly, you'll need to think about your pots and pans: Nearly all the methods we've looked at require them to come into contact with an open flame and that's very different from cooking on an electric burner.

Durable Cookware

First, for any open-flame cooking, be that over a campfire, over the embers of your wood-burning stove, or on the barbecue, you're going to need a grill. You can get these in various sizes, so make sure you get something that's big enough for your family's needs but small enough to suit your heat source. I have a couple of camping grill grates from Redcamp which are made of stainless steel and about as easy to clean as a grill can ever be. Any brand will be fine, though: Just make sure it's durable and certified as safe for use with food. I also have a campfire grill, which is a much better option for an open fire. It's conveniently foldable and it stands over the flames like a table so you can easily set a pan of water over it without worrying about putting your fire out.

With the grill covered, you want to turn your attention to cookware. Your main goal is durability, so I'd recommend cast iron, stainless steel, or aluminum. They all have their advantages and disadvantages, and I think ultimately, I'd recommend having a bit of everything if you can. It just gives you more flexibility in terms of the types of food you can cook and how. Stainless steel has the advantage of being easy to use and it's great for using over moderate heat. It's not as good for cooking over an open fire where the temperature is high, though, and it's hard to clean the outside of a stainless steel pan. Aluminum isn't great for very high temperatures either but it does have the very definite bonus of heating up quickly, so used over a camp stove, it can help you conserve fuel. Cast iron is renowned for its weight and durability and I'd say this is really your best option for open-fire cooking. If you want to keep costs to a minimum, skip the aluminum and focus on cast iron for open flames and stainless steel for less intensive cooking.

FUELING THE FIRE

Many of these cooking methods require fire, so stocking up on fuel and fire-lighting tools should be a solid part of your preparation plan. This is part of the reason it's so important to decide what cooking methods you plan to turn to in advance and practice using them. You need to know exactly what stocks you need so that you can be confident that you really do have an emergency backup option.

Exactly what you need to stock up on depends, of course, on what devices you need to fuel. But regardless of the details, I'd recommend having plenty of matches and lighters on hand. These will always be useful and I'm not sure it's possible to have too many. That said, I'm a firm believer that the best thing you can stock up on is knowledge, and knowing what to do if you run out of matches or lighter fluid is a peace of mind I know I want to have.

So, let's make sure you know how to get a fire going even if your stocks dry up.

Emergency Fire Lighting

There are four primary ways you can start a fire without matches: friction, sparks, the sun, or chemicals. I mention chemicals only so that you're aware of all the options but I'm not going to look at that too closely here. I don't like the idea of stocking potentially hazardous materials if I don't have to and you can easily start a fire without resorting to using them.

There are multiple ways to use friction, sparks, and sunlight but here we'll just look at one solid option for each approach.

Friction

While friction may be the first thing that comes to mind when you think of starting a fire, it's actually one of the most difficult approaches. Using a hand drill is probably the simplest option available to you but this can be tricky in wet conditions. Begin by cutting a V-shape in a piece of board and making a small depression beside it. Place a bit of bark beneath the notch in order to catch the ember when it lights. You'll now need a spindle about 2 feet in length. Place this in the depression, and roll it between your hands while moving them up and down the spindle with speed and pressure. Keep going until the end of the spindle glows red and an ember is created. Now tap the board to knock the ember onto the piece of bark, and then use it to spark a bundle of tinder. This will quickly go out if left alone, however, so you'll need to blow on it to generate a flame.

Sparks

To use sparks to start a fire, flint and steel is probably the most straightforward method. You can actually buy kits to save you searching for the right materials, which might be a worthwhile investment if you're not used to the process. I've used these, and I have to say they're easier than trying to use found objects. The spark is created when the hard flint is struck with the relatively soft steel.

Begin by holding a piece of hard rock (the flint) between your forefinger and thumb, allowing the sharp edge to stick out a couple of inches. Next, you'll need to lay some char cloth against the flint. Use the steel to strike the flint using a quick wrist movement. You'll need to do this a few times but you will find that sparks will begin to fly at the char cloth fairly quickly. Once it begins to glow, you can transfer it to a pre-prepared nest of tinder and then wrap the nest with the char cloth. Again, you'll need to blow on it to get a flame going. You could also add dry twigs and grass to encourage it along. Once you have a steady flame, you can transfer the bundle to your fireplace, which should already be laid with logs.

Sun

Harnessing the power of the sun to start a fire works by concentrating a sunbeam onto a particular material but it's only really an option in bright, clear weather. The most obvious way to do this is to use a magnifying glass, preferably one that will allow you to rotate it rather than one with a handle. This will give you greater control and allow you to change your angle as necessary. Lay your tinder on the ground, and use the magnifying glass to direct the sunlight onto it. Keep the angle steady, and slowly you should begin to see smoke rising from the tinder nest. As soon as that happens, it's time to blow on it until you have a flame.

FUEL CONSERVATION TECHNIQUES

No matter how much fuel you've stocked up on, you're going to need to use it wisely to make sure it lasts for as long as possible. Mostly, what this comes down to is mindful cooking, by which I mean paying close attention to how you're cooking each food. This begins by using the right equipment for the job. If your wood stove is already burning to heat the house, this is a logical place to boil your water as it won't require using any additional fuel. On the other hand, if all you want to do is boil that pan of water and the stove isn't being used for another purpose, you'd be better off using your camping stove. Think about what fuel you're already using and consider whether you can also use it for cooking. If not, ask yourself which is the best tool for the job.

When you're cooking, aim to cover your food as often as possible. This prevents heat loss by keeping the steam in the pan and cooking its contents more quickly. Of course, there are times when keeping the steam in the pan isn't going to work for the type of meal you're cooking, so use your discretion. Another trick is to cut your food into smaller pieces in order to speed up the cooking process. Think of cooking a jacket potato in the oven versus frying small pieces of potato over a burner: If you have an open fire going anyway, baking potatoes in foil packages is a good use of fuel; if not, you'll use less fuel if you opt for small chunks of potato fried over a camp stove.

Of course, a few of the cooking techniques we looked at also lend themselves naturally to fuel conservation. Any time you can use solar energy for cooking you're essentially getting free fuel, and if you turn to thermal cooking, you'll be using no fuel beyond what is required to get the dish started. One method we didn't look at, however, was pressure cooking. This is often seen as quite an old-fashioned way of cooking but in a grid-down situation, it will really come into its own. If you want to cook dried beans, for example, a pressure cooker will allow you to do this in just a little more time than it takes to warm up a pan of cooked beans. As a result, you'll make significant savings in fuel—particularly if you then finish those beans off using thermal cooking techniques.

GRID-DOWN COOKING SAFETY

It's easy to focus on the ways you can cook as normally as possible in the event of a power outage without giving a second thought to safety. But this will need to be at the forefront of your mind as normal safety mechanisms won't be in place, and you'll often be working with dangerous tools and substances.

The main thing is really just to be aware of the hazards. If you're using gas, carbon monoxide is always a risk so it's important to have a detector. Any open flame is also a danger. It's obvious, but it's something the whole family needs to be aware of. Make sure the kids know to stay a safe distance from the fire and make sure everyone knows how to use a fire extinguisher. My attitude has always been to get the kids involved in everything. That way, you teach them the skills while also building a natural awareness of safety. Obviously, you want to keep very little ones away from the cooking action but once they're old enough, I think the best way to keep them safe is to let them understand what you're doing, how you're doing it, and how you're making sure you're doing it safely.

SOURCING FOOD

I'm assuming that you're coming to this book with a lot of things already in place for an emergency situation, and that includes a well-stocked pantry. If you still need more information on this, have a look at my last book, *The Prepper's Pantry*. One thing I'd like to add here, though, is that it's a good idea to stock up on some foods that don't require cooking. This will help you conserve fuel, and it means you'll always have an option if everything doesn't go to plan with your cooking arrangements.

Hopefully, your stocks will see you through the length of the disaster, but the reality is, if the grid goes down in a big way, we just don't know what the future's going to look like. I want to look at a few other ways of procuring food for that reason, but bear in mind that whole books can be written on this and you'll definitely need to do further research.

Gardening

The reason your pantry is so important during a grid-down situation is that food supplies are going to be hit hard. If you have the space to grow your own food, I'd say that's really the best thing you can do to ensure your family has a steady supply of nutritious food. Of course, you can't account for every disaster, and if the reason the power's out is due to extreme weather, the chances are your garden's going to take a knock. But getting a vegetable garden started now is going to serve you well in most situations, so if you have the space, I'd say it's definitely worth researching and adding to your project list.

Keeping Livestock

Keeping livestock isn't a possibility for everyone and if you live in an urban or suburban area, there may well be zoning laws preventing it. Space is also an issue for many people. Nonetheless, protein is an important dietary requirement, and animals and animal products provide it in abundance, so if it's an option for you, it's worth considering. Chickens, ducks, rabbits, and goats are all good options but you'll need to do your research carefully and make sure you know what you're doing before you get started. Animal welfare is crucial, and you'll need to know how to recognize signs of sickness and make sure you know what to do about them. You'll also need to learn skills in butchery and safe meat preparation. I'm certainly not suggesting it's an easy task, or even one that will suit everyone, but if you have the space and time to invest in the project, it would be a great asset in a grid-down situation.

Hunting

If you're not able to keep your own animals, it doesn't mean that fresh meat isn't available to you, but again, you're going to need to train up well in advance of an emergency. If you're already a seasoned hunter, you're one step ahead of the game, but bear in mind that hunting in a grid-down situation could look a little different from what you're used to. You may not have gas to fuel your car, so bringing a deer home might be challenging. You may need a little more knowledge about the habitats and behaviors of your prey. You may even need to resort to some unusual animals: Trapping animals like raccoons, rats, and beavers could become necessary in an extreme survival situation.

It's also crucial to keep safety in mind. If you live in a densely populated area, this is probably still going to be the case in an emergency, so shooting ducks at the local pond isn't necessarily a safe choice. If you do intend to add hunting to your skill set, I'd recommend taking a survivalist hunting course to make sure you know exactly how to hunt safely and exactly what equipment you need to have on hand.

Foraging

It blows my mind that we don't forage more. There's so much food around us that we're often not even aware of. The problem is, some plants are highly nutritious but others are poisonous, so foraging is a risky business if you don't know what you're looking for. I think a book on edible plant identification is an incredibly worthwhile investment for any household that wants to be prepared for the worst. We have a couple and we've actually had some brilliant family days out searching for food in the wild and then coming up with ways to use it.

Foraging can be split into two main categories: urban foraging and wilderness foraging. Wilderness foraging is probably the kind you naturally think of: searching for foods that are readily available in the wild. Your best bet is to buy a book and get to know what grows near where you live. Everything from crabapples and pine nuts to berries and mushrooms is a possibility.

When it comes to urban foraging, this comes down to what's available in your city. Community gardens are an obvious source of fresh food but beyond that, you need to tune into your apocalypse movie mindset. Think abandoned grocery stores, restaurants, vehicles, and dumpsters. It's a bit grim perhaps, and hopefully not something you'll ever have to resort to, but I find there's a bit of comfort in thinking through all of these possibilities and knowing where you can turn in an emergency.

Your pantry is a crucial part of your survival plan but it's of limited use if you don't know how to use it. That means making sure you have alternative cooking methods ready to go as soon as they become necessary... and it means practicing all to a proficient level.

TAKE ACTION: MAKE A CROSSBOW

I did think twice about including this section but in the end, I decided that if you're not a seasoned hunter, having the skills to make a DIY crossbow would be a definite bonus, and I know you'll have fun with this one.

A crossbow is essentially a hunting weapon made up of a horizontal bow attached to a stick (known as the stock). It is used to shoot bolts at a target, and if you have good aim, it's an efficient way of making a catch.

What You Need

- Pine wood, 2-inch thickness
- Pine wood, 1-inch thickness
- Nylon string
- Varnish or wood stain
- Wood glue
- 36-inch length of 1-inch PVC pipe
- 2 x wood screws
- 2 x pulleys
- Wire tires
- Nylon string
- Duct tape
- Nails
- Foam padding
- Dowels (if you want to make your own bolts)

The Mission

Step 1

Begin with a 2-inch x 2-inch pine board that is approximately 38 inches long. This will make your stock. Gripping this in your hands while pressing one end to your shoulder, find a comfortable size for your bow. Mark this length and saw off the excess wood.

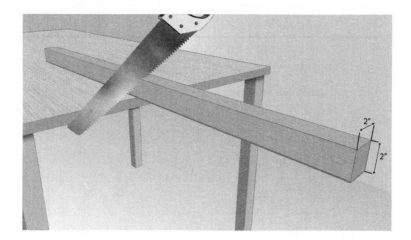

Step 2

Lift the wood up into a crossbow position again, pressing one end to your shoulder as you did before. Now make a mark on the top surface of the wood where it would feel comfortable to have a handle and trigger. On top of this mark, draw a rectangle around 4 x 1 inches in size.

Step 3

Taking care not to split the wood, gouge out the rectangular area with a drill, a chisel and a wood rasp until you have a clean hole. Smooth the surrounding area with sandpaper. This is your trigger hole.

Step 4

Now make a groove about ⅛-inch long by the front of the trigger hole using a chisel. Sand the area well. This is where the string will lie across the trigger hole.

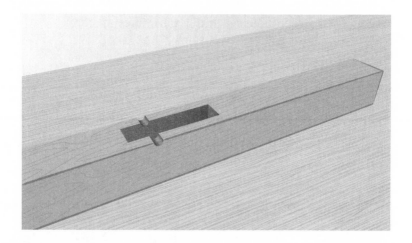

Step 5

The next step is to make a groove to hold the bolt, which will reach from the trigger hole to the end of the wood. On the opposite end of the wood from the string groove, make a mark in the center. Now mark the center of the end of the trigger hole at the end furthest away from the string groove. Join your two marks with a straight line, and then use a hammer, chisel, and drill to make a channel around ¼ inch deep. Sand this area well.

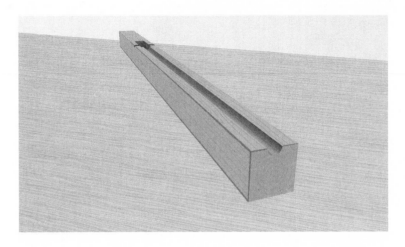

Step 6

You now need to make a grip that you can use when you're shooting. You'll need a second piece of wood for this, cut to a length of 8 inches. Glue this to the bottom of the stock and allow it to dry thoroughly.

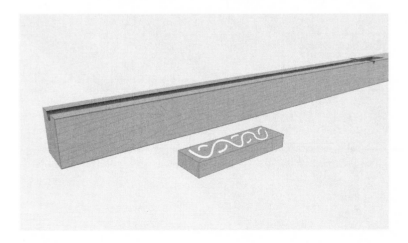

Step 7

Varnish the stock, or use a wood stain to protect it from the weather.

Step 8

To make the bow, you'll need a 36-inch length of 1-inch PVC pipe. Cut a groove into either end of this large enough to hold a small wood screw.

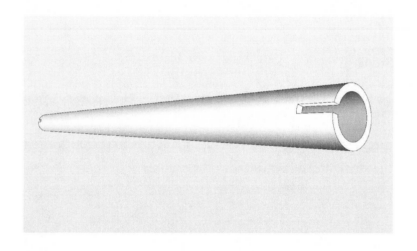

Step 9

Now put a small wood screw into each grove and attach a pulley to each one with wire ties.

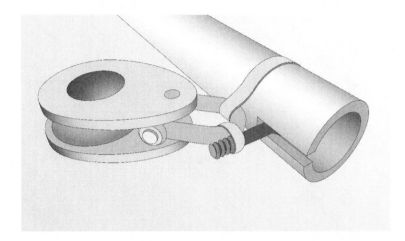

Step 10

Fasten one end of a piece of nylon string to the screw on the left-hand side of the pipe, and then loop the opposite end around the pulley on the right-hand side. Now bring the string back to loop around the left-hand pulley, before taking it back to the right-hand side and tying it to the wood screw. A quick word of caution here: Be careful not to pull the string taut when you wrap it around each pulley, otherwise you won't be able to pull it and operate the crossbow. The string should now be running across the pipe 3 times, and it should be secure but not tight. You can test this by pulling on the string. If the pipe flexes, the tightness is correct. Otherwise, you'll need to rethread the pulleys.

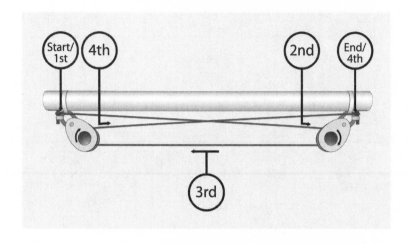

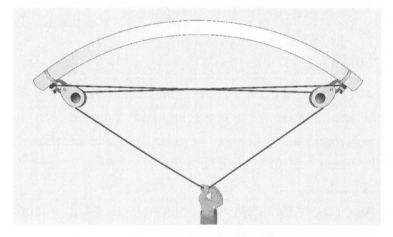

Step 11

Return to the stock, and use a chisel to carve out a groove that the pipe will fit into snugly. It should have no space to slide around.

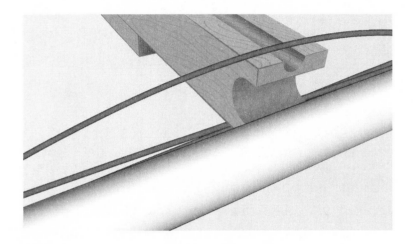

Step 12

The bow will now need to be attached to the stock with the strings in the right place. Attach the pipe to the stock securely with duct tape. Make sure that there is only one string on top of the wood (this is the firing string). The other two strings should be underneath the wood.

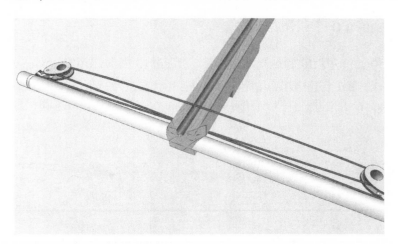

Step 13

Test the bow by drawing back the firing string and securing it in the string groove you made earlier. If it won't stay in place, you'll need to make the notch deeper.

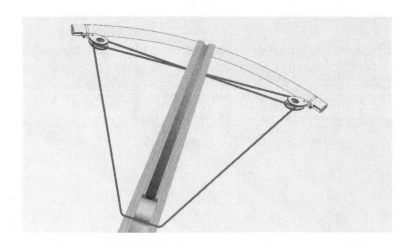

Step 14

Sketch out a rough L-shape on a new piece of pine wood, ideally about 1 inch thick. This will be your trigger system. The bottom line that makes the L should be a little smaller than the rectangular hole in the stock. Cut out the L-shape and sand it until the edges are smooth.

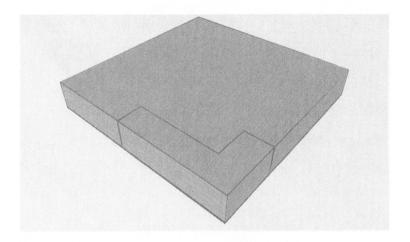

Step 15

Carve a channel, about ⅛ inch long, across the shortest side of your L-shape using a chisel.

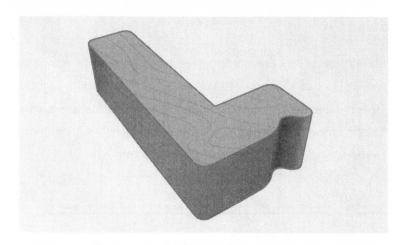

Step 16

In the center of the L's corner, drill a hole big enough to hold a nail. This is how the trigger will be fixed to the stock.

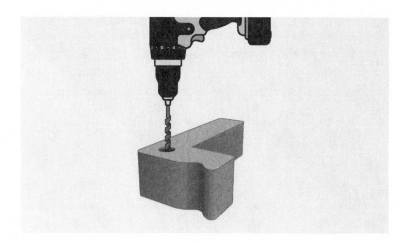

Step 17

Your aim is to fix the trigger to the stock so that when it's pulled, it will push the string out of its groove. Place the trigger in the rectangular hole so that the L is pointing forward and the groove is facing upward. It should have space to move without touching the back of the trigger hole. Hammer a nail into the stock, holding the trigger in place.

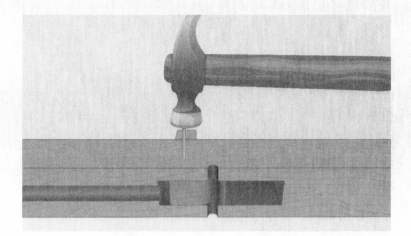

Step 18

Ensure a smooth firing action by sanding the trigger down thoroughly.

Step 19

You're now going to make a handle so you can hold your crossbow steady while you pull the trigger. Cut an 8-inch piece of pine wood into a rough handle shape and refine it by sanding it down.

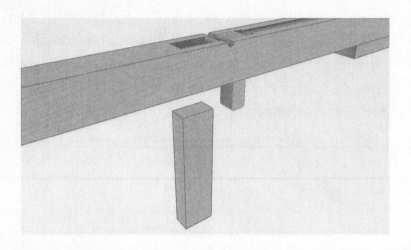

Step 20

Glue the handle onto the stock behind the trigger. Leave this to dry completely and then strengthen the join with nails.

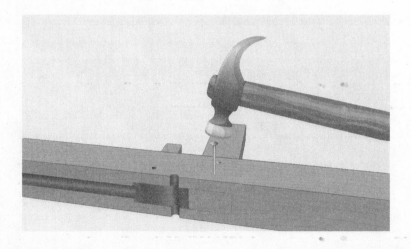

Step 21

In order to make the crossbow more comfortable to use, pad the end that will press against your shoulder with foam and secure this with duct tape.

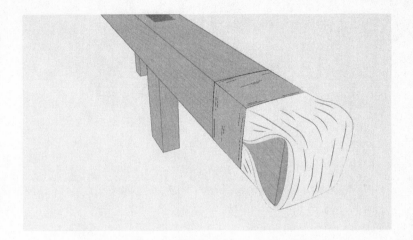

Step 22

You can always buy bolts from a hardware store, but you could also make your own using dowels. To do this, cut dowels down to fit the channel on the crossbow, making notches at the ends to grip the string.

Step 23

You now need to test your crossbow, so set up a target and find a safe space to try it out. It could fire bolts to a distance of 100 feet so make sure you test it somewhere with lots of space.

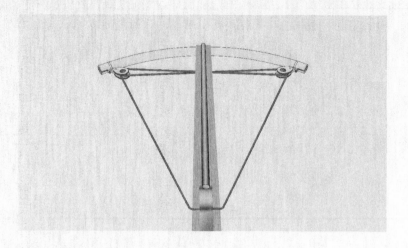

It's Time to Channel Your Inner Athlete!

If you aren't going all the way, why go at all?

— JOE NAMATH

Athletes can tell us a lot about survival. There's something about the competitiveness of pro sports, the utter determination, strength, and resilience you need to make it to the top, that mirrors the attitude you need to survive an emergency.

I'd hazard a guess that some of the people best equipped to thrive in a grid-down emergency are elite athletes. I'm pretty sure Joe Namath is going to be fine... and not least because he knows what it means to be part of a team.

When I think about that quote, I don't think about football... I think about preparedness.

If you aren't going all the way, why go at all?

If you're preparing your home for a disaster, why stop short of preparing for a grid-down situation? I know I had to look at my own plan carefully... I hadn't gone all the way. And, truth be told, I still haven't – and I won't have until I know I've done everything possible to get this information out there.

So I want to take a sliver of inspiration from Joe... and I want to bring you along for the ride. I want us, together, to go all the way. To make this journey really worth it, we have to bring as many people along as possible. It's not just about my family surviving. It's not just about your family surviving. It's about the whole team.

And I'm going to need your help.

In order to get this information to as many people as possible, we're going to need to spread the word. It's not enough for us to be the athletes; we have to be the coach and the cheerleaders as well.

So here's what I'm asking: Would you be willing to leave an honest review of this book on Amazon?

Every review will bring our community one step closer to what they're looking for.

When we work together, we truly can go all the way... and I can't thank you enough for joining forces with me.

We're healthy; we're strong; we're prepared... Let's make sure we all stay that way!

8

LONGER-TERM SOLUTIONS

MEDICAL CARE

I could devote a whole book to medical care, so I'd like to start out by making the disclaimer that this chapter is designed to give you the basics. I have to admit, when I was researching it, I realized that my own stockpile was somewhat lacking in the emergency health department. I had medicine and first aid covered, but I'd neglected to include useful ingredients that could be used for first aid in an emergency. Needless to say, I've remedied this now and it is my hope that by the end of this chapter, you'll have a better understanding of what you need to have in your home to ensure peace of mind in an emergency.

I covered basic medical and first aid supplies in my first book, *When Crisis Hits Suburbia*, so I'm going to assume that you have the basics covered. That way, I won't have to repeat things you already know. However, for those of you who are just getting started, the *Take Action* section at the end of this chapter is a first aid kit checklist—so don't worry if this is still all a bit new to you.

MINIMIZING RISK

Before we get to essential supplies, let's take a step back and look at how you can minimize risk in the first place. There are four main categories that we can split this process into preventative medicine, infection control, injury prevention, and disease management.

Preventative Medicine

Crisis or not, the health of our families is always at the forefront of our minds and we have a duty to make sure we're making lifestyle choices that support our physical and mental health. That means a good diet and regular exercise, and it means keeping up with medical and dental appointments. Of course, if the grid goes down, those appointments might not be possible but by staying on top of your health now, you run less risk of these being necessary during an emergency. What you can also do is make sure your pantry is stocked with nutritious long-life foods that will provide you with all the nutrients you need to stay healthy and strong no matter what's going on outside.

Infection Control

The next layer of reducing risk is to keep infection at bay as far as possible. The best way you can do this is to make sure the whole family is washing their hands, not just regularly but often. If the causal agent behind grid disruption is a pandemic, use what you learned when Covid-19 broke out in 2020: If you go out, wear a face covering and wash your hands as soon as you come back home. Keep a safe distance from others and if you suspect that you or someone in your family has been infected, keep everyone at home.

Infection control is still important even when there isn't a pandemic at work. In any crisis, we'll be collectively producing a lot of waste that may not be disposed of in the usual way. This provides the ideal breeding conditions for bacteria, so be mindful of managing waste safely (we'll look at this more closely in the next chapter) and keep washing your hands often.

Injury Prevention

Infection isn't the only risk to your health: Injury is also a possibility and in a grid-down crisis, getting medical attention is probably going to be very difficult. Taking active steps to reduce the risk of injury is, therefore, vital. What this mostly comes down to is being aware of everything in your environment and the risks they pose. In an emergency situation, avoid areas where you're more likely to run into danger and avoid being out on your own after dark. Do your best to avoid confrontation, and if you're out and about and sense that tempers are rising, abandon your mission and head home.

At home, you want to make sure you take extra steps to protect your family's safety around emergency backup plans for heating, lighting, and cooking. Make sure you have key safety equipment like fire extinguishers and carbon monoxide detectors, and make sure your walkways are lit well enough that you can see where you're going as you're navigating your property.

Disease Management

If you live with a chronic disease, part of being prepared is to plan for how you intend to manage it in an emergency scenario. Physicians will usually write prescriptions for 90 days if you ask them, and this is worth doing so that you have essential medications in backup. You'll also want to stock up on any foods, supplements, or alternative medicines you rely on for the management of your condition. If you generally attend physiotherapy appointments, make sure you're aware of the exercises you can safely do at home if this service becomes unavailable to you.

MEDICINE TO STOCK UP ON

Stockpiling medicine is a little more sensitive than stockpiling food. Although most foods have a limited shelf life and you have to think about this when you're stocking your pantry, you can generally build up a bigger supply than you can with medicine. Most medicines have a relatively short shelf life, and it's important to aim not to use them past their expiry dates (although you can afford a bit of flexibility when you have no other option).

Building Your Stockpile

The best way to start is to think about the needs of every member of your household. Consider whether anyone in your family has allergies to any pharmaceutical products. Does any member of the family have a chronic condition that needs to be accounted for? How about seasonal allergies? Acute pain? You want to consider your family's daily needs and not just possible emergencies. When I did this for my family, I made a spreadsheet to make sure I could track everyone properly. I'm a big fan of spreadsheets but a word of caution: If you're the same, make sure you have a hard copy of all vital information. Those spreadsheets won't bring you peace of mind in a grid-down situation if you can't log onto your computer.

The next thing to think about is quantity. You'll need to plan for the worst and figure out the amount of medication you'll need to take care of your family, and then add a little more to be on the safe side or share with others as necessary. Stocking over-the-counter medication is fairly easy: You can probably keep enough to last for a good couple of years. But with prescription medication, while your doctor may be willing to write a script for a longer supply, you're unlikely to be able to get more than enough for a few months. And of course, you can't just buy all your supplies and forget about them: You'll need to restock every few years to make sure that you're only keeping medicine within its expiration date.

Medicine Shelf Life

I would always recommend paying attention to expiration dates and making sure your stockpile is as fresh as possible. That said, in an emergency situation, it's helpful to know how safe some of those older medications are. When they're stored properly, many medications are still very effective for a good five years after their expiration date. They will, however, lose potency with time, so the older a medication is, the less effective it will be. Liquid medicines are also likely to deteriorate more quickly than those in tablet form. If you find yourself in an emergency situation with only medication that is past its date, make a judgment based on its appearance. If it's still the same color and it hasn't visibly deteriorated, it's most likely safe to take. If tablets stick to each other, are chipped or cracked, or are softer or harder than they should be, give them a miss. Of course, it *is* a risk, and not one I would take unless it was essential.

Storing Medicine Safely

The best way to ensure that your medicines are still safe to use even if they're a little past their expiration dates is to store them properly. That means keeping them in a cool, dark place, out of the reach of sunlight. You might think the medicine cabinet in your bathroom would be the best spot but it's actually a fairly bad idea, especially for long-term storage: The humidity and heat in your bathroom aren't good for medicines. Storing your medical supplies in the same place that you store your food is a good idea, as long as you can still keep them safely away from children. And a little extra security measure: Consider locking prescription meds in a safe. In an emergency situation, those drugs are going to be very valuable, and not just to those who need them for medical conditions.

Essential Medicines for Your Store Cupboard

I can't tell you exactly what your medical supplies should look like: This will be very personal to your family's unique needs and that's why thinking it through carefully is so important. What I can do, however, is provide you with some hints for a strong foundation. There are probably a few things that it would be good to have in an emergency that you don't already have in your first aid kit.

Pain medication/fever reducer: Over-the-counter pain relief is useful for a whole range of potential issues, including fatigued muscles, headaches, and minor injuries, so it makes sense to have plenty on hand. Acetaminophen is a good choice for treating both pain and fever, while ibuprofen and aspirin also work to reduce inflammation. Bear in mind, however, that children shouldn't take aspirin. I'd opt for a liquid medicine for younger children but remember that this won't keep for as long as tablets.

Anti-diarrheal: Not many people keep an anti-diarrheal medication in their regular medicine cabinet but you won't necessarily be able to run out at the last minute if the grid goes down, and diarrhea is not what you want to contend with in an emergency, not least because it can lead to dehydration. You've got two options here: a thickening mixture to absorb water or an antispasmodic to slow down activity in your lower intestine. Loperamide is a good option for this.

Oral rehydration solution: I'm including this here because if someone does have diarrhea and becomes dehydrated, an oral rehydration solution is a helpful tool. You don't need to buy this though: You can make your own by dissolving 1 teaspoon of salt and 7 teaspoons of sugar in a pint and a half of boiling water and allowing it to cool.

Constipation relief: At the other end of the spectrum is constipation, which is a risk if your food stocks dwindle and you struggle to get enough fiber. It can also be a problem if your diet changes slightly or if you're stressed, and both of these things are highly possible in a grid-down situation. An osmotic laxative like Polyethylene Glycol 3350 is a good choice, as well as glycerin suppositories for quick relief.

Antibiotics: In the case of a bacterial infection, you'll want to have antibiotics on hand (either in tablet form or as a topical cream) if you can get hold of them, but you'll need a prescription, which may be tricky if you don't have an immediate need. Hopefully, they won't be necessary, but it's possible that you'll cut yourself at some point, and the last thing you want is to have no way of treating it if it becomes infected. Remember that antibiotics don't have any effect on viruses though, so they're useless for colds, the flu, and the majority of sore throats and coughs.

Colloidal silver: I'm mentioning colloidal silver because many preppers firmly believe it's a necessity, but there's a lot of debate around it, so read up carefully to decide if it's right for you. It's a strong natural antibacterial, antibiotic, antiviral, and antifungal treatment, and can soothe everything from burns to boils. It doesn't require a prescription, which is why so many people favor stocking it, and it may be a good alternative to fall back on in an emergency.

Cough drops: I don't really know what I can say about cough drops, apart from, "Get some!" They're cheap enough and a cough is irritating at the best of times.

Antihistamines and anti-itch cream: An over-the-counter antihistamine is a good idea to have on hand to fight the symptoms of seasonal allergies, itching, respiratory infections, and hives. Diphenhydramine is a good option and it has the added bonus of reducing anxiety and relieving insomnia, both of which are perhaps a bit more likely in a grid-down situation. A topical anti-itch cream is a good idea too.

Ammonia inhalant: Basically a fancy way of saying "smelling salts," an ammonia inhalant is designed to revive people who have fainted. Hopefully, you won't need it but having some on hand will bring you peace of mind.

Specialty drugs for specific risks: We've discussed the importance of stocking up on prescription medications but it may also be a good idea to think of the potential crises that could cause a grid-down situation and stock medication for these scenarios too. There are two main areas I'd look at here: a nuclear event and a pandemic. If there was a nuclear disaster, radiation would be a risk, so potassium iodide tablets are a good measure to take. These will prevent radiation from being absorbed by your thyroid gland. The specifics of a pandemic cannot, of course, be predicted but you can stock a couple of antiviral medications that may help. You will need prescriptions for these, but if you're able to get hold of them, oseltamivir or zanamivir (used for the treatment of influenza) are a good idea.

NATURAL MEDICINE

Although some medicines may be usable after they've passed their official expiry date, medication does have a shelf life and we have no idea how long a potential disaster could go on for. That makes some knowledge of herbal remedies essential, in my opinion, and there's a whole world of possibility out there when you open yourself up to it. I have to admit, since I started looking into natural remedies myself, I've got the bug for it. You'll find whole books out there dedicated to herbal remedies. All I've done here is compile a list of some of the ones I think may be most useful in an emergency situation. Some of these are stock cupboard staples; others you may want to grow at home or find in supplement form from a health food store.

Aloe vera: This spiky little plant has huge healing powers, especially when it comes to treating skin and burns. It's also helpful for the digestive system and immune health. You can grow it at home or you can buy it as an essential oil.

Echinacea: Echinacea stimulates the production of white blood cells and increases your ability to fight infection. It's great for the common cold, a sore throat, or bronchitis, and it also has anti-inflammatory properties which can help with arthritis. To ease a sore throat, add around 15 drops of essential oil to a cup of water and use it for gargling.

Elderberry: As well as making a mighty delicious cordial, elderberry is helpful to the immune system and has been shown to be effective against avian and swine flus. You can grow it and use the berries or you can buy capsules.

Honey: Is there a better way to start the day than with a hot piece of toast loaded with honey? Even better when you find out how powerful honey is. If you can resist eating it and use it as a topical application instead, it has skin rejuvenating and antibacterial properties. And when you eat it, it has huge benefits for your gut health. The only thing is, a lot of the honey on the shelves is very processed, so to get the most beneficial product you'll need to spend a bit more and opt for natural, raw, organic honey that hasn't been pasteurized. Ideally, you want Manuka honey, which is thought to be the most healing, but this can be very expensive.

Peppermint oil: A cup of peppermint tea can help with soothing cramps and muscle spasms, it can ease a headache, and it can be used to help with sinus infections. You can also use it externally for pain relief by applying it to a damp washcloth and laying it over the affected area.

Apple cider vinegar: If you have an apple tree you can make your own apple cider vinegar, but it's readily available in most stores if not. It's great as an energy booster and it can help with digestive problems, as well as having topical applications for first aid.

Salt: The chances are you already have plenty of salt in your pantry, but were you aware of its healing properties? It plays an important role in balancing your electrolytes and therefore supporting muscle function. It also helps with digestion and aids in recovery when you're sick. And as if that wasn't enough, it has dental benefits and antibacterial properties, making it a good addition to a gargling solution for sore throats.

Garlic: Garlic is loaded with goodness and has strong antibiotic and antiviral properties. When ingested, it's very good for gut health and soothing oral infections but it has topical applications too. A crushed clove of garlic spread onto a piece of gauze and applied to a painful area is surprisingly helpful. It can reduce joint pain, as well as soothing earaches and toothaches.

Coconut oil: Coconut oil has huge nutritional benefits when ingested but it also has oral benefits when used as a mouthwash, and it can be used topically to improve dry skin conditions. If you're planning on making balms or ointments using other natural ingredients, it makes the perfect base.

Cayenne pepper: This is a powerful tool in the fight against disease prevention, and surprisingly enough, it also has healing powers when applied topically to a wound. If you suffer from arthritis, you can dilute cayenne extract in dimethyl sulfoxide (DMSO) and use it as a topical treatment. Added to hot water, it can also help with digestive issues or it can be added to a gargling solution to soothe a sore throat.

Chamomile: If you've ever had trouble sleeping you've probably tried a comforting mug of chamomile tea before bed, and there's a reason it works. It's a mild sedative, and it can help to calm the mind and body. It can also help with indigestion, menstrual cramps, and morning sickness. Soaked flowers can also be used in a warm compress to soothe ear infections and eye problems.

Dandelion: A highly misunderstood plant, dandelion has a number of health benefits. It can reduce cholesterol levels and stabilize blood sugar, and it can also reduce the symptoms of gout. The chances are you already have plenty in your backyard, even if you aren't intentionally trying to grow it.

St. John's wort: Another plant that grows abundantly in the wild, St. John's wort has antibacterial and anti-inflammatory properties and can soothe wounds when applied topically. It can also be used to treat hemorrhoids, relieve joint pain, and reduce anxiety and fatigue.

Marigold: If you're a gardener, marigold is a helpful companion plant, and if you're growing it for this reason you have a wealth of bonus health benefits up your sleeve. It can be used on the chest along with peppermint to reduce a fever, and it can be steeped in water and combined with apple cider vinegar to make a tonic to be applied topically for inflammation relief. It also has healing properties when applied to an open wound.

Thyme: Apart from being delicious, thyme is a powerful little herb. It can help with gastric problems, soothe a sore throat, and be added to tea to treat a fever. It also has benefits to the nervous system and can help to soothe a headache. When used topically, it's useful for treating skin conditions like eczema and psoriasis and can also be used to treat burns and infections.

Sage: Sage has antiseptic properties and can be used to improve oral health. A sage bath will also help to bring down a fever and sage tea will soothe stomach problems and ease flu symptoms.

Nettles: I'm not sure if there's a more maligned plant than the stinging nettle, but as much as it hurts to brush up against one when you're out walking, this is a plant with some powerful properties. Nettle tea can be an effective solution for reducing allergy symptoms, and, bizarre as it may seem, it can also treat skin conditions. It can relieve joint and muscle aches and increase immune function, and it has benefits to urinary and prostate health.

A basic knowledge of herbal medicine, a well-stocked medicine cabinet, and some essential first aid skills are all going to be essential in a grid-down crisis. If you're not confident in your first aid skills, now's the time to enroll in a basic first aid course. I make sure I refresh my knowledge regularly, and I've made sure my whole family knows the basics too. If the grid goes down, medical help may not be readily available, so it's up to us to do what we can to protect our families.

TAKE ACTION: EMERGENCY FIRST AID KIT CHECKLIST

Besides your medications and herbal backups, you want to make sure you have all the essential first aid tools in stock. I covered this in *When Crisis Hits Suburbia*, but I've made this checklist a little more comprehensive. Use this list to make sure your first aid kit is up to scratch.

- ☐ Medical tape
- ☐ Nitrile gloves
- ☐ Rolled gauze
- ☐ Gauze pads
- ☐ Trauma shears
- ☐ Liquid bandage
- ☐ Moleskin
- ☐ Abdominal gauze pads
- ☐ Butterfly bandages
- ☐ Chest seals
- ☐ Z-fold gauze
- ☐ Coban roll
- ☐ Pressure dressing
- ☐ Band-Aids
- ☐ Styptic powder
- ☐ Tourniquets
- ☐ Splints
- ☐ Tweezers
- ☐ ACE bandages
- ☐ Rubbing alcohol
- ☐ Peroxide
- ☐ Saline eye drops
- ☐ Irrigation syringe
- ☐ Plastic wrap
- ☐ Safety pins
- ☐ Emergency blankets
- ☐ Thread and needle stored in isopropyl alcohol

9

LONGER-TERM SOLUTIONS

SANITATION AND HYGIENE

As we saw in the last chapter, prevention is one of the best ways to make sure your family stays healthy in an emergency, and a big part of prevention is maintaining hygiene and sanitation without the support of the grid. Perhaps you remember the 2010 earthquake in Haiti: It was followed by an outbreak of cholera which resulted in a huge number of deaths. This is exactly the sort of thing we want to avoid, so we need to make sure we know how we're going to deal with personal hygiene and waste in the event of an emergency.

ESSENTIAL SANITATION SUPPLIES

Let's start with the supplies you're going to need in your stockpile. I'd recommend stocking enough supplies to last a year, so first you'll need to calculate how much of everything you use. This is easier than it sounds: Just scribble the date on every new package you open, and when you finish it, make a note of how long it lasted. Every household is different, so you might have things you want to add or remove from this list, but this is what I'd recommend as a basic starting point:

- Toilet paper
- Reusable washcloths (emergency toilet paper)
- Cleansing bottle (makeshift bidet)
- Baby wipes (for cleaning up without water)
- Soap
- Hand sanitizer
- Shampoo
- Toothpaste
- Toothbrushes
- Dental floss
- Deodorant
- Dishwashing liquid
- Laundry detergent
- Disinfectant
- Disposable gloves
- Feminine hygiene products
- Garbage bags
- Diapers (if applicable)
- Quicklime (for toilet safety)
- Appropriate chemicals to keep chemical toilet running (if applicable)
- Rodent poison/traps
- Insect repellents

TOILETING

It's not the most pleasant thing to think about, but it's one of the most important things to get right in an emergency situation. Every member of your household generates about 5 gallons of human waste per week. If you have no running water, disposing of it is going to be an issue, and if it's not managed properly, it can pose a danger to your family's health. While urine is relatively safe, feces can spread disease, so it must be managed correctly in order to prevent odor, disease, and illness.

Flushing with Water

When You Have a Septic System

If you have your own septic system, you have an advantage if the grid goes down. As long as you have access to water, be that water you've stored or water you've collected, you'll be able to flush your toilet. You'll simply need to fill the cistern until the water hits the float and then flush as normal. Alternatively, you could pour a 2-gallon bucket of water into the toilet bowl, which will trigger it to flush on its own. Word of advice though: Your water is precious, so don't flush unless you really have to. A friend of mine likes to say, "If it's yellow, let it mellow," which I think is great advice in this situation. There's no harm in a few people using the toilet before you flush if it's only urine. Even if you do have a septic system, however, I'd recommend coming up with a contingency plan, just in case something goes wrong or you run low on water.

When You're on a Sewer Line

Most septic systems have been replaced now and the majority of households are connected to a sewer line. What you'll need to do if this applies to you is check that the sewer main hasn't gone down. If it has, avoid flushing your toilet—this will protect your plumbing from backing up and stop sewage from coming up into your sinks and toilets. If there's no problem with the sewer line, however, you can top up your cistern with water and flush as though you were on a septic system—as long as you have enough water to do so.

Alternative Toilet Options

Regardless of whether you have a septic system or not, I would recommend having a backup plan that doesn't involve water at all. Water is going to be a precious resource in a grid-down situation, and personally, I'd be wary of using too much of it for the toilet. The good news is that you have plenty of options, but the best one for you will depend on whether you live in a rural or an urban environment.

Rural Settings

If you live in a rural area (or even a suburban one with plenty of space and privacy around your home), outdoor toileting is going to be a good option for you in a grid-down emergency.

Cat Hole

A cat hole is really better for a short-term crisis than it is for a long-term one but it's worth knowing about, and it will make a good temporary measure while you're sorting out a longer-term solution. It's not something you can do once and then use again and again though: You'll need to dig a new hole each time someone wants to use the toilet.

Use a trowel or a shovel to dig a hole about 8 inches deep and about 6 inches wide. Use the hole as a toilet, and bury your waste with the dirt you removed to make the hole. It's super easy but you should keep a few rules in mind before you start digging holes all over your backyard. Your cat hole site shouldn't be within 200 feet of a water source, and you should avoid digging your holes anywhere that water is visibly flowing. Aim to spread your cat holes out as far as possible and try to dig in an area that's exposed to a lot of sunlight to encourage decomposition.

Trench Latrine

In the event of a long-term crisis, a trench latrine is a better solution. It's essentially a giant version of a cat hole that can be used repeatedly. You'll need to follow the same rules as you do for cat holes, keeping it away from your water source or any flowing water and aiming for a sunny spot, if possible.

This time, you want to dig a trench around a foot deep, spanning a length of about 2 feet, and with a width of about 1 foot. I would take a bit of extra time to build some sort of privacy barrier too, which can be as simple as a piece of tarp or an old sheet stretched between stakes in the ground. Your family will be using the trench regularly, so flies and pests may be an issue. Keep them off your waste (and keep odor to a minimum) by covering it with quicklime or wood ash after each use. Once your trench is half full, add a layer of quicklime and then fill in the hole with soil. Build this up into a mound so that there's an extra foot of earth covering the surface. You'll then need to dig a new trench.

Deep Pit Latrine

A trench latrine is better than a never-ending string of cat holes in a longer-term emergency, but if the crisis goes on for a long time, a better option would be a deep pit latrine. Think of Roman toilets—the wooden seats placed over a deep pit. That's essentially what you're going for. You want to dig a hole about 6 feet deep, 2–6 feet long, and 2 feet wide. Make a seating area from whatever materials you have available, and construct some kind of shelter or privacy barrier as you would for a trench latrine. You'll still need to sprinkle quicklime or wood ash into the trench after each use, and the pit will need to be covered once it's full to within a foot of the surface, just as with a trench latrine. The good news is that when you dig your new trench, you won't need to make a new seating area—you can just reuse the original one. Make sure the new pit is the same size as the first one though, or you run the risk of the seat collapsing into the trench.

Urban Settings

If you live in the city or a densely populated suburban area, you probably don't have the land you'd need to dig latrines, so you'll need to consider other options. Luckily, there are a few ways around the problem.

Permanent Porta Potty

Even if you're not able to flush your toilet, you can still use it in an emergency; you'll just have to repurpose it a little. Start by turning off the water supply to the toilet and removing as much water as you can from the bowl, and then tape a double layer of heavy-duty trash bags to the bottom side of the toilet seat. After using the toilet, cover the waste with a layer of ash, quicklime, or sawdust to control odors. Once the bag is ⅔ full, add a generous amount of quicklime, tie the bag up, and replace the lining in the toilet. Keep the lid down when the toilet's not in use but bear in mind that odor will still be a problem when you can't flush. Combat this by covering the whole toilet with a 30-gallon trash bag when it's not in use.

Bucket

Okay, so it's not glamorous, but a bucket makes a perfectly serviceable toilet if you double-line it with heavy-duty trash bags. To make it more sanitary, mix a cup of liquid bleach with 2 quarts of water and add this to the lining, adding a bit more bleach after each use. Don't let the bag get over a third full before changing the bag. You can either perch on the rim of the bucket, or you can remove the toilet seat from your toilet and use this over your bucket. You can actually buy toilet seat covers especially made to fit 5-gallon buckets, so that's an option too. If the smell is a concern, you can get toilet deodorants to control the odor.

Chemical Toilet

The advantage of chemical toilets is that you can flush after every use, they reduce the risk of disease spreading, and the chemicals help with odor control. They have a removable bucket so you can dispose of the waste safely, but if you opt for one of these, you'll need to make sure that your stockpile has enough of the right chemicals to keep you going through an emergency.

Commode

Anywhere that sells medical supplies will sell bedside commodes and they're really useful in an emergency. They have an easy-to-empty bucket and they often have an adjustable seat height. You'll need to use liners with them, which typically come with an odor neutralizer, decaying catalyst, and gelling agent to reduce the risk of disease and control odors.

Composting Toilets

You might see these called biological toilets, waterless toilets, or dry toilets, but they all amount to the same thing. They convert human waste into soil or fertilizer by allowing the organic matter to break down into its essential minerals. Word to the wise, though: You can't use the resulting compost on your vegetable garden. You only want to use it on land where you're not growing food. Composting toilets are a more expensive option but they're certainly one to consider, and they're perhaps the best option when it comes to minimizing odor.

PERSONAL HYGIENE

Frequent handwashing is one of the most important things your family will need to do to keep healthy during a grid-down crisis. Make sure you do this before every meal, after each time you use the toilet, and after doing any other manual task. Water conservation is important but it's still possible to be clean and comfortable, even when you have to be mindful of water use.

Keeping Clean without Running Water

The most important thing to keep in mind is that your purified water should be used for drinking, cooking, and doing the dishes before it is used for anything else. Any water you do decide to use for washing can be recycled for other purposes, such as flushing the toilet or watering plants. If you live near a stream, river, or lake, you have access to free washing water. If you do this, however, make sure you use biodegradable soap (which you can also use for washing in the rain).

If you don't have access to rivers and lakes, and it doesn't rain regularly where you live, you still have options. You could use a spray bottle to minimize the amount of water you're using, or you could use damp washcloths and sponges, baby wipes, or a sanitizing lotion. Just make sure you have all these things in stock and make sure you have a dedicated area reserved for sanitation. If you're at home, your bathroom will still probably be your best option, but if you have more than one bathroom and you'll be using an indoor toileting system, I'd suggest using one bathroom for washing and one for going to the toilet.

Alternative Bathing Solutions

While minimal-water sponge baths and river bathing are adequate enough to maintain personal hygiene, if the grid is down for any length of time, you will want a more comfortable option, and there are some make-shift bathing options you have at your disposal.

Gravity Solar Showers

A surprisingly cheap option is a gravity solar shower, which essentially works when you warm water up in the sun and then use it for showering. A black shower bag is left to sit in the sun for a few hours and a showerhead is then used to shower in the usual way. Most of the gravity solar showers I've seen have a 5-gallon capacity which is probably about enough for two showers.

Pressure Tank Garden Sprayers

You could also use a pressure garden tank sprayer in a similar way: The tank is left in the sun to warm up (or you could heat your water separately and then fill the tank). These sprayers have various kinds of nozzles, but for showering your best option is to look at sporting stores. They often carry sprayers designed specifically for showering.

Tubs and Cowboy Baths

Baths will obviously use more water but you could go old school and use the same water for the whole family. This is how baths were traditionally used among ordinary working folk. Remember that you'll need to heat your water first before filling the bath.

A less water-intensive version of this is the cowboy bath. For this, you heat the water and keep it in a bucket beside the bath, and then pour it over yourself while you're sitting in the tub.

WASTE MANAGEMENT

The final piece in the sanitation puzzle is waste management. With garbage collection being a standard part of daily life, it's easy to forget how much waste a household produces, but once collections stop, you'll soon see that it's significant. The problem is that garbage attracts pests and diseases, so you'll need to have a plan in place in case garbage collection comes to a halt.

Separating Waste

Start by separating your waste into things you can burn, wet trash, and recyclables like glass, plastic, and cans. If you leave these things mixed together, the wet trash will contaminate everything else, and wet trash breeds bacteria and attracts pests.

Reducing Bulk

You then want to make your trash as small as possible, which you can do by flattening boxes, squashing cans, and compacting whatever you can. You want to make sure you have plenty of high-quality trash bags on hand, and ideally, a few lidded trash cans.

Composting

If you have the space for one, composting is a good idea, even if you don't have a garden to fertilize, as it's a hygienic and efficient way of disposing of organic waste. You can compost kitchen scraps, shredded cardboard and paper, and yard waste, as well as manure from non-meat-eating animals. You want to set up your compost heap as far away from your house as you can because, as hygienic as it is, it will attract insects. If you don't have a compost bin, cover your compost heap with black tarp to speed up decomposition, and be sure to turn the pile regularly.

Burning Trash

Some garbage can be burned and although this may not generally be the most environmentally-friendly choice, it may be necessary in a grid-down situation—and it means you have free fuel for cooking. You can burn cardboard, paper, and packaging like cereal boxes and cook safely over the fire. And to really make the most of your resources, you can use the cooled ashes for odor control in your latrine (alternatively, these could be added to your compost heap). Make sure you know what can safely be burned though: Never burn Styrofoam, plastic, or other items that could release toxins.

Burying Trash

If the crisis goes on for a long period of time, it may become necessary to bury some of your garbage. If it comes to this, bury it as far away from your house as you can. You'll need to dig a hole about 4 feet deep and cover your trash with around 20 inches of soil (this will keep pests away). If you want to dig a hole and keep filling it before you're ready to cover it, lay a large piece of wood over the top, and weigh it down with rocks to keep pests out. If you're using the same hole for multiple bags of trash, I'd recommend layering it with quicklime or ash to keep odors to a minimum.

PEST CONTROL

No matter what care we take with our sanitation, it's important to keep pest control in mind at every stage. All the waste generated by your household is liable to attract pests and this can put your supplies at risk.

To prevent insect infestations, keep garbage disposal areas as clean and as far away from the house as possible, and try to avoid having areas of standing water as this encourages mosquitos. Keep lids on trash cans closed, cover food and crockery, and keep insect control devices like fly strips and fly swatters on hand. Make sure all your food is packaged carefully and stay on top of your laundry (we'll look at this in the next chapter).

Your other threat is rodents and keeping these guys away can be a little more challenging. I'd recommend storing some traps and poisons just in case. Keep your storage areas clean and make sure all your food supplies are packaged properly. Mylar bags can be tempting when you're storing food for an emergency but rodents can easily chew through these, so if you're using them, I'd recommend storing them in plastic buckets or boxes.

Sanitation and hygiene are crucial to safety in an emergency situation, and if the grid goes down, the ways this is usually handled will fall by the wayside. Make sure you have a plan in place to keep personal hygiene and waste management in check if the worst happens.

TAKE ACTION: DIY HAND SANITIZER

Although you'll still need to have the supplies to make it, you can make your own DIY hand sanitizer, and to me, hand sanitizer means peace of mind when the water's off. All you'll need are isopropyl alcohol, aloe vera gel, and tea tree oil. Combine 3 parts isopropyl alcohol with 1 part aloe vera gel, and add 3–5 drops of tea tree oil to improve the scent. You could use a different essential oil for this if you're not a fan of tea tree oil.

10

LONGER-TERM SOLUTIONS

LAUNDRY AND DISHWASHING

L aundry and dishwashing are really a part of sanitation and hygiene but I wanted to separate them to make it all a bit more manageable. Keeping your clothing and bedding clean, and making sure your kitchen hygiene is as close to your usual standards as possible, is important for your family's health and safety. We'll start with dishwashing, and the good news is that if you've ever been camping, you probably already know exactly what you need to do.

DISHWASHING

The lack of running water means you can't rely on your kitchen sink, so I think the best plan for a grid-down scenario is to use the three-sink dishwashing method used by campers, which is probably easiest done outdoors if the weather permits.

Essential Kit

Here's what you'll need to set up an efficient and hygienic dishwashing station.

- 3 buckets/dishwashing bowls/camping sinks
- Sponges/brushes/scouring pads (for washing)
- Chamois cloth (for drying quickly)
- Biodegradable dishwashing detergent
- Bleach or Steramine tablets
- Metal strainer

The System

Start by removing all solid food from your dishes and scraping off as much wet residue as you can. Heat enough water to half-fill all three buckets and cut this with cold water until you reach a comfortable washing temperature. Your aim is to create a washing sink, a rinsing sink, and a sanitizing sink. The washing sink should contain warm water and dishwashing soap, the rinsing sink should be filled only with warm water, and the sanitizing sink should contain warm water and your sanitizing agent (use 2 teaspoons of bleach or 1 Steramine tablet per gallon of water).

Begin with the cleanest dishes, washing each one in the wash sink before dunking it into the rinse sink to remove all suds. Then soak your dishes briefly in your sanitizing sink to ensure they're completely disinfected. It may be tempting to overlook this step, but it's particularly important if any of your dishes or utensils have come into contact with raw meat or fish.

You then want to towel-dry your dishes with your chamois cloth. Once everything is washed, consolidate your gray water into one bucket, and strain the food particles out with your metal strainer. The food waste will go in with your wet garbage, and the water can be disposed of. If you're able to use the drains, this can be poured directly down, but if everything's blocked, you'll need to throw your water away outside. Try to spread it over a large area in this case, and don't dispose of it within 200 feet of a water source.

LAUNDRY

Laundry is a little more challenging than dishwashing, but it's just as important. If you're able to connect it to a water supply, you can use your backup power source to run your washing machine, but washing machines take a considerable amount of power and water, so personally, I'm not sure that doing this is the wisest move. Luckily there are quite a few alternatives available to you, but the bad news is that they mostly involve a bit of elbow grease.

Manual Methods

We'll start off with the most labor-intensive options. These approaches to laundry don't require electricity and use minimal water and they're the methods used before the washing machine was invented. When I think about the inconvenience of doing laundry this way, I try to remind myself that this was what the generations before us had to do all the time. For all of these methods, the best bet is to make your own detergent, simply because commercial brands tend to leave you with a lot of suds, and they're going to be hard to rinse out without a machine. The good news is, that's an easy task: See the *Take Action* section at the end of the chapter for details.

Wash Basin and Washboard

The washboard method was used for centuries and while it's hard work, it's an effective way of getting clothes clean. Washboards were originally made from metal and wood, but nowadays you can get silicone ones too. You'll need one of these and three buckets of warm water: one for washing and two for rinsing. The idea is to apply soap to both the washboard and any large patches of dirt on the fabric. The clothes are then scrubbed up and down on the board until they're clean. Each garment must then be soaked in the first rinse bucket and rinsed thoroughly, before being transferred to the cleaner water in the third bucket for a final rinse. For particularly dirty garments, you may want to soak them overnight to boost the chance of removing any stains.

Bucket and Brush

The bucket and brush method is essentially the same kind of deal, but it involves scrubbing with a brush rather than against a washboard. Prepare a wash bucket with warm water and laundry soap. Immerse each garment thoroughly, soaking them for longer if necessary, and agitate them to mimic the motions of a washing machine. Then use a soft-bristled scrubbing brush to scrub the most soiled areas. As with the washboard method, each garment will then need to be rinsed thoroughly in two separate rinse buckets.

Plunger

I really like the plunger method because it's a little less back-breaking than the washboard or brush methods. You can buy plungers specifically designed for laundry (The EasyGo Washing Wand is a popular example), or you can just use an ordinary toilet plunger. The slight advantage of specifically-designed laundry plungers is that they have holes in them, which means the water is pushed out and sucked back through, resulting in a more thorough wash. You'll need a bucket filled with warm water and laundry soap, and the idea is to mimic the action of a washing machine by pushing and pulling the plunger to agitate the laundry for around 10 minutes. You'll then need to rinse it in your separate rinse buckets, or for particularly dirty items, you may want to let them soak overnight before rinsing.

Sailor's Method

The sailor's method is particularly useful for larger items like sheets and blankets. You'll need a heavy-duty trash bag (ideally black because the idea is to use the sun to warm the water) filled with water and laundry soap. The idea apparently comes from the way sailors would wash their clothes on voyages: The sun would warm the water and the movement of the ship would agitate the clothes. You don't have a ship to do this for you but you can get the same effect by pressing and moving the bag. Once you've agitated the laundry for around 10 minutes, you'll need to rinse it using the two-bucket method we've discussed.

Powerless Washing Machines

Before you get too excited, powerless alternatives to washing machines still require a fair amount of work, but they're a little less labor-intensive than the more old-fashioned methods.

A Wonder Washer is essentially a hand-cranked washing machine, designed to take around 5 pounds of laundry. You simply add your laundry load, fill up the machine with warm water and laundry detergent, and mix it using the built-in levers. One of the best things about these is that you don't need the extra buckets for rinsing because you can just drain the soapy water and then add clean water to rinse. Personally, I think one of these is well worth the investment, particularly if you think you might struggle with the more labor-intensive hand-wash methods (you'll still need to be able to turn the lever around 200 times though, so it's not as easy as putting a load on and making a cup of tea). There are other models that do the same kind of job as the Wonder Washer too— I've heard good things about the Avalon Bay Eco Wash and the Laundry POD, for example.

Powered Washing Machines

You have two options when it comes to using some of your power for laundry: the wringer washer and an energy-efficient regular washing machine.

Wringer Washer

Wringer washers were popular after the war, and work in a similar way to a regular washing machine. Many Amish families still use them with their diesel generators, and you'll be able to use one of these with any backup power source you're using. They have an accessory for wringing garments out after washing but you'll want to buy a separate spinner, as they tend not to be that efficient.

Energy-Efficient Washing Machines

If you do want to use a washing machine during a long-term grid-down crisis, you'd be better off with an energy-efficient washing machine. If you're intending to use a machine in an emergency, I'd recommend looking into the most energy-efficient appliances you can find so that they don't drain your power. The wringer washer will use less power than a standard energy-efficient washing machine but they do still require you to wring out the clothes, so you may prefer a completely hands-off approach. Even with the most energy-efficient model, however, this is only really an option for you if you have a strong source of backup power.

The Extra Steps

Unless you're able to use a machine, laundry is going to involve a few more steps than you're used to.

Rinsing

We've touched on rinsing in all of the manual methods, so you already know about the two-bucket rinse system. When you're doing this, you'll also need to agitate the laundry, just as you did at the washing stage. This will release the suds but you'll end up with suds in your water, which is why the second bucket is necessary. If you're opting for the plunger method, using the plunger to agitate the clothes will make rinsing easier. If you're using a Wonder Washer or similar device, you can simply refill it with clean water for rinsing after your initial wash. Just don't be tempted to skip this step.

Wringing

You don't necessarily need to wring out your load after rinsing, and there is a school of thought that says it's better not to as it can stretch the fabric. However, it does speed up the drying process considerably, so unless you have delicate items that are more likely to stretch, it's probably worth doing. You can wring each garment out by hand, but that will require a fair amount of effort, and it can get tedious by the time you get to your sixth shirt. An old-fashioned wringer where you turn the handle to press the water out of the clothes will be worth the investment if you don't fancy spending a whole day squeezing water out of clothes.

Drying

If you're used to drying your clothes in a machine, you'll need to change your plan if the grid goes down. Dryers use a considerable amount of energy, so it wouldn't be wise to plug a dryer in when power conservation is so important. Your best bet is to hang them on a line outside. Even in very cold weather, your laundry will dry eventually, but this can take a full day, so you may want to hang it on a drying rack in whichever room you're heating instead.

Tips for Taking the Torture Out of Laundry

There's no way around it: Laundry during a grid-down crisis is going to be more difficult than usual and I doubt any of us are going to love it. Here are a few hacks to keep the torture level to a minimum.

The first thing I'd suggest is making sure you shake out each garment before washing it. This will mean that your washing water stays cleaner for longer and avoids debris getting stuck to other items. To be honest, we do this at home anyway, mostly because my kids are incapable of putting a pair of pants in the laundry hamper without checking the pockets first, and it does help get rid of large pieces of dirt.

The next thing I'd suggest is soaking your laundry before you wash it, even if it isn't particularly soiled. Again, this will keep your washing water cleaner for longer, and it'll also mean that any dirty patches you haven't noticed will require less effort once you get to the washing stage. With manual methods, your hands will really thank you for any corners you can cut along the way.

I've mentioned warm water throughout this section, and I think that's probably the most effective approach. It's also more pleasant if you're washing by hand. That said, if you need to conserve energy, don't panic if you need to wash in cold water. Your laundry will still clean this way. There is one garment where heat is necessary though: underwear. For personal hygiene reasons, you want to make sure underwear is as clean as possible and the easiest way to achieve this is by boiling it. Place your undergarments in a pot of water and bring it to a boil over your fire or stove. Be very careful not to burn it though and don't put too many garments in at once. They should have room to float in the water without touching the sides.

I can't say I'm looking forward to doing laundry in a grid-down crisis, but there's no denying that it's a necessity. It'll take water and a lot more manpower than you're probably used to, but it will be possible to maintain high laundry standards without the grid.

TAKE ACTION: DIY LAUNDRY DETERGENT

Making your own detergent will make rinsing your clothes a lot easier than it would be with commercial soap. All you need to do is mix 1 cup each of borax, Fels-Naptha soap, and washing soda; scent the mixture with an essential oil (if you like); and seal it in an airtight container. You'll just need 1 teaspoon of detergent per 5 gallon wash.

11

LONGER-TERM SOLUTIONS

COMMUNICATION

I f the grid goes down, it isn't just your computers that will go dark: It's your cell phone too. Communication is often overlooked when we think about preparedness, but being able to keep in touch with your loved ones and keep on top of changing information will be vital in an emergency situation, no matter what the cause.

During the initial stages of a power outage, cell phones should still work, at least for a few hours. Cell towers do rely on power, but most will have a backup system that will allow them to operate for a few extra hours. Landlines, however, might fare a little better. They are powered by the phone lines, which means that if the main grid goes down, they may still work. It's not a failsafe by any means, but if you've done away with your landline in favor of your cell phone, I'd think about getting it reconnected. It could make a huge difference in an emergency. Bear in mind, though, that if you opt for a cordless phone, these do still need power.

Nevertheless, extreme weather and other disasters can easily bring phone lines down, so you'll need some backup communication plans in place too.

GOTENNA

Being able to keep in touch with your family within the local area is probably the biggest communication priority, and the goTenna is a useful tool for this. When attached to a smartphone, it enables you to create a short-range network. This can span anything from half a mile to a few miles, but it largely depends on the terrain of the area. Even if the cell towers are down, a goTenna will allow you to call and text your family and local friends if someone needs to leave the group for whatever reason. They are quite pricey though, so you may prefer to use another option.

CB RADIOS

Citizens Band radios, or CB radios, are pretty easy to get hold of, but they have limitations. They're most frequently used by truckers for short-range communication, they're not that expensive, and you don't need a license to use them. Like the goTenna, they have a limited range, so while they'll be great for staying in touch with your family in the local area, they won't be so helpful if you need to go further afield. Not all that many people use them, so to make them worthwhile, you'd need to get one for every member of your household, and even then, you may not be able to tap into emergency station frequencies. That said, there's a low barrier to entry with the CB radio and if you know that other people in your area are using them, it could be a useful addition to your communication plan.

FRS/GMRS

Other options are Family Radio Service (FRS) or General Mobile Radio Service (GMRS) radios. Both kinds use UHF frequencies, which usually have a short range of around a mile. You don't need a license to operate an FRS radio, and you can have different conversations on one channel because of the privacy codes they're programmed with. Nevertheless, the short range again makes them better for a small group staying within a localized area.

GMRS radios are less accessible as you do need a license to use them, but they have a lot more power and a lot more uses. A license isn't all that expensive, and it remains valid for five years, but individuals have to be licensed separately. It is technically possible to run an unlicensed station, so if your license runs out, you could still potentially use your radio in an emergency when licensing laws are not a priority. Don't go into this with this in mind though: Always stay on the right side of the law and get any necessary permits. Using an unlicensed radio should only ever be a backup option in an emergency. The power range is much stronger than the FRS radio, and if you use a removable antenna and a repeater you can extend the range to around 30 miles (depending on the terrain). Some channels overlap with FRS frequencies, which means you can pick up a wider range of benefits with the GMRS radio.

SATELLITE PHONES

Satellite phones have a lot of potential in an emergency but they're not without their drawbacks, the main one being that they rely on satellites—so if the satellites stop working, so do the phones. They're also quite costly, not least because you need to pay for the service and the time you spend using it as well as for the phone itself. Nevertheless, they're a great option. The least expensive approach is to opt for a device that sends short text messages and is able to transmit your location. You can get satellite phones with much greater capabilities than this but the more your phone does, the higher the costs are. I have a Garmin Inreach Explorer and I'd definitely recommend it. Get your practice in on Twitter though:

You can only send text messages up to 160 characters long, so you'll need to get used to being succinct. If you'd rather have a device that also allows voice communication, I've heard good things about the Inmarsat IsatPhone 2, which can make calls across the globe and will work in extreme weather conditions. I'm considering getting something more comprehensive like this, but they're expensive, so weigh your options carefully.

HAM RADIO

I'm not sure there are many communication devices as effective as ham radio, but this is something else you need a license for. I got my Federal Communications Commission (FCC) license not all that long ago and I'm really happy I did. Ham radio can reach far out of your local area, which is why they're so commonly used by search and rescue teams. Using one means you'll be able to keep updated on the crisis by tuning into emergency stations, and you'll also be able to stay in contact with your loved ones. Despite the requirement for a license, ham radio is actually more common than CB radio, so the chances of being able to contact people outside of your household are greater. They take a bit of practice, it has to be said, but if you're studying for your license anyway, you'll get that practice in. The barrier to entry is quite high because the licensing tests are quite science-based and you do need to study to acquire the necessary knowledge. I enjoyed it though, and if you can handle it, I'd still recommend getting a license. Expense-wise, there's quite a range with ham radios. The more you get into it, the more you're likely to spend on accessories and equipment, but at a basic level, you can access what you need to without spending too much.

WALKIE TALKIE

Walkie talkies have their limitations, but they're great for local use and they're dead simple, so they're great if you have children. No licenses are required and they're battery-operated, so as long as you have plenty of AA batteries in stock, you should be fine in an emergency. Like the CB radio, however, the range is very short, so you can only really use them in a localized area. That said, to keep in touch with family and neighbors over short distances, they're a great asset. We have them in our house and the kids like to use theirs when they're playing outside. I've always encouraged this on the grounds that it might make a real-life emergency a little less daunting for them.

POWERING COMMUNICATION

Whatever devices you intend to use, you'll need to factor in what you need to power them. Make sure that when you're taking an inventory of the batteries you need to stock up on, all communications devices are accounted for. A quick word on batteries though: They don't last forever and they lose power over time. Just because your devices have fresh batteries in them now, doesn't mean you can assume they'll still be fine in a year's time. Check your supplies regularly, and make sure you refresh them as needed. If you plan to use a solar charger, make sure this can connect to your communications devices or batteries.

It's easy to forget about communication in an emergency situation because we have such good communications in place in regular life, but if the grid goes down, keeping in contact with your family and local community is going to be invaluable. Having a way to access emergency stations and keep on top of updates is also going to be crucial. If you're considering ham radio, make sure you get a license and learn the skills in advance. Even if the license becomes irrelevant in a crisis, you'll need it to use and learn ham radio now, and that's something you'll need to do long before a disaster.

TAKE ACTION: KNOW THE EMERGENCY FREQUENCIES

Whatever radio system you're using, you're going to need to know what emergency stations to tune in to. This is by no means an exhaustive list of the emergency frequencies, and you'll definitely want to research the ones in your local area too. However, I suggest making a chart like the one below and printing it out to keep with your emergency devices so that you know you can always tune into emergency updates in a crisis.

RADIO	STATION	FREQUENCY
CB RADIO	PREPPER CB NETWORK (AM)	CHANNEL 3 (26.984 MHZ)
CB RADIO	THE AMERICAN PREPPERS NETWORK (TAPRN)	CHANNEL 4 (27.005 MHZ)
CB RADIO	UNIVERSAL CB EMERGENCY/REACT CHANNEL	CHANNEL 9 (27.065 MHZ)
CB RADIO	COMMONLY USED ON CAMPGROUNDS AND IN MARINE AREAS	CHANNEL 13 (27.115 MHZ)
CB RADIO	SURVIVALIST NETWORK	CHANNEL 36 (27.365 MHZ)
CB RADIO	PREPPER 37 USB	CHANNEL 37 (27.375 MHZ)
HAM RADIO	EMERGENCY FREQUENCY FOR NATIONWIDE NATIONAL GUARD	34.90
HAM RADIO	POLICE INTER-DEPARTMENT EMERGENCY COMMUNICATIONS	39.46
HAM RADIO	NATIONWIDE RED CROSS CHANNEL	47.42

HAM RADIO	FEMA* DISASTER RELIEF CHANNEL	138.225
HAM RADIO	EMERGENCY FIRE DEPARTMENT CHANNEL	154.265
HAM RADIO	POLICE INTER-DEPARTMENT EMERGENCY COMMUNICATIONS	39.46
HAM RADIO	NATIONWIDE RED CROSS CHANNEL	47.42
HAM RADIO	EMERGENCY FIRE DEPARTMENT CHANNEL	154.28
HAM RADIO	EMERGENCY FIRE DEPARTMENT CHANNEL	154.295
HAM RADIO	USED DURING SEARCH AND RESCUE	155.160
HAM RADIO	POLICE EMERGENCY COMMUNICATIONS	155.475
HAM RADIO	INTERNATIONAL MARITIME WEATHER UPDATES	156.75
HAM RADIO	NOAA**	162.40

HAM RADIO	NOAA	162.425
HAM RADIO	NOAA	162.45
HAM RADIO	NOAA	162.475
HAM RADIO	NOAA	162.50
HAM RADIO	NOAA	162.525
HAM RADIO	NOAA	162.55
HAM RADIO	NOAA	163.275
HAM RADIO	EMERGENCY COMMUNICATIONS FOR THE NATIONAL GUARD	163.4875
HAM RADIO	MILITARY NATIONAL DISASTER PREPAREDNESS	163.5125
HAM RADIO	FEDERAL GOVERNMENT CIVILIAN AGENCIES EMERGENCY AND DISASTER FREQUENCY	168.55

HAM RADIO	NATIONAL COMMUNICATIONS FREQUENCY FOR THE DEPARTMENT OF STATE	409.625
HAM RADIO	GENERAL MOBILE RADIO SERVICE EMERGENCY COMMUNICATIONS AND TRAVELER ASSISTANCE	462.675

*FEMA: FEDERAL EMERGENCY MANAGEMENT ASSOCIATION (FRONT LINE OF LARGE-SCALE DISASTER RESPONSE)

**NOAA: NATIONAL OCEANIC AND ATMOSPHERIC ADMINISTRATION (GOVERNMENT ADMINISTRATION FOR SENDING OUT EMERGENCY BROADCASTS)

You can download a printable version by scanning the QR code below.

LONGER-TERM SOLUTIONS

SECURITY

I covered security in *When Crisis Hits Suburbia*, so again, I'm mindful of repeating information. Nonetheless, it's worth recapping the three Ds of security: detect, deter, and defend. These are the three basic principles to work with when it comes to protecting your home, with defense being the final line of protection. Hopefully, if you have detection and deterrence in place, you'll never have to get to that stage. And when it comes to a grid-down emergency, the good news is that a lot of your measures don't need to rely on the grid anyway, so if you have all of this in place, you shouldn't need to worry about too much extra.

SEEING THROUGH THE EYES OF AN INTRUDER

If you're starting to think about security for the first time, I think the best approach is to look at your property through the eyes of an intruder. You can actually make this into a fun game with the whole family (my kids loved donning balaclavas and creeping around the house like ninjas for the afternoon!)

Start from the street around dusk when the light begins to wane. Think about what you can see through the windows. Are there valuables on display? Could someone watching the house see what was going on inside? Next, think about the landscape around your property. Are there places for someone to hide? Would it be easy for someone to hop the fence? Consider what you could do to make your home seem less appealing to intruders. If you're really getting into the spirit, you can challenge your kids to get into the house (without breaking anything) without using their key or any key codes you may have. I was sure my family wouldn't be able to get into our house. We have no key under the doormat or anything, and I was sure everything was secure, but my son was able to pry open a window that I didn't realize I'd left open—it was quite an eye-opener.

Take notes on any weak points you noticed and start thinking about what you can do to strengthen your property. Would more secure fencing be a good idea? Do you need to upgrade any windows or doors? Perhaps some net curtains would be a valuable asset for hiding the contents of your living room. It's amazing what insights you can get simply by viewing your home through the eyes of someone who might want to break into it.

OFF-GRID SECURITY

If you have intruder alarms or security cameras that rely on the grid, you may need to think more carefully about your non-grid reliant security, so it's worth reviewing a few key points here.

Layers of Protection

I think it's helpful to think of home security in layers, starting by making your property a less appealing target. Remember that your main priority is to protect the people who live in your home. After that, it's precious supplies and resources. Personal possessions are the last thing to worry about, although of course, you want to make sure they're safe too if you can. A quick word of warning though: You don't want your home to be so secure that escaping it is difficult. In an emergency, your family needs to be able to get out quickly and easily.

Start by thinking about the appearance of your home. Consider valuables that may be on view both inside and outside of the property. The more you can hide from view, the less attractive your home will be to intruders. Aim to blend in with your neighbors' properties, and try to make your home look secure without seeming like a fortress that could be protecting huge assets. You want to stay under the radar but still look secure enough that no one is tempted to break in just because it will be easy.

Barriers

Perhaps the best thing you can do to protect your property is to minimize the risk of an intruder getting to it in the first place. And a good way to do that is to create barriers—most likely in the form of fences. I know some people talk about making these fences hostile by using barbed wire or electrification but I have two thoughts that put me in the camp against doing this. First, although some of you may live in rural areas, there's a high chance that you live in the suburbs where this kind of defense simply isn't safe in regular life. Second, if you have children, your job is to protect them and make them feel safe, and if they're playing out next to an electrified fence, this isn't going to do that. And the icing on the cake is that if we find ourselves in a grid-down situation, that electrified fence is going to be pretty useless. Personally, I think a tall, solid fence is all most people need to provide an effective barrier. I think we need to find the balance between protecting our homes and living a full and peaceful life.

Alarms

If you have intruder alarms, it may be that they're currently reliant on the grid, so you'll need to think about what to do to mitigate this should the grid go down. The good news, however, is that you can switch to solar or wind energy to power your alarm system. Alarms have two benefits: First, they deter criminals as soon as they're triggered, and second, they alert you to the presence of an intruder. The even better news is that you can easily create an off-grid alternative that doesn't require power at all.

One of my favorite DIY alarm systems is the good old cans-on-a-wire setup, which simply involves stringing empty cans on a wire, close enough together that they'll rattle if they're knocked. This should be semi-hidden behind some foliage above ground level. The only problem with this is that high winds can trigger a false alarm. An electronic system is probably more reliable if you're able to hook it up to your alternative power source.

Lights

Lights work in a similar way to alarms to deter intruders, but they do rely on electricity. If you're generating power through wind or sun, you should be able to power some intruder lights; alternatively, you could power them through deep-cycle batteries. There are three approaches you can take to lighting: You can opt for an always-on approach, you can have them only on at certain times (i.e., only at night), or you can have them activated by movement. Movement-activated lights make for good deterrents but the problem is that they can just as easily be triggered by animals as they can by people, so they're not always a reliable alert. The added problem in an emergency is that if the reason the grid is down is due to extreme weather, they could easily be triggered or damaged by those conditions.

Dogs

We have three dogs, none of them trained solely as guard dogs, but they would still be a real asset if there was an intruder trying to break in. Most breeds don't require much training to want to protect their territory or their family, and even a good bark can be enough to deter intruders. In a grid-down event, the fact that dogs don't require electricity is a definite bonus—although there may be times you might wish you could power them down for an hour! If you're considering getting a dog, bear in mind that each animal you have is an extra mouth to feed, and weigh this carefully against the benefits to security.

Traps

I'm not of the mindset that having traps permanently set up around your property is a safe way to live, particularly if you have children or pets. Nonetheless, if we find ourselves in a crisis situation, there may come a time that setting up a few traps will be a good way of adding an extra layer of protection to your security system. If you're genuinely concerned about a threat to your property, you can set up snares using heavy-duty steel wire. These won't cause permanent harm to the intruder but they will make it difficult for them to get closer to your home or to escape if they get caught. The other advantage, of course, is that traps like this may also snare you some small game, which could be a valuable source of food. Double-check the zoning laws in your area before setting up any kind of trap. Small snares like this will probably be okay in most areas, but if you were considering something more serious like a bear trap, you may find that there are laws against this. At the very least, you'll need to display warning signs on your property.

Reinforced Doors

With deterrents in place, you can then move your attention to more localized barriers. A good starting point is to think about the strength of your doors. You can boost your security significantly simply by reinforcing the doors you already have in place, and this isn't as hard as it sounds. All you need to do is replace the short screws fixed into the strike plate with longer screws that can pass through the frame and screw into the stud—3-inch screws would be a good call for this. You can also replace any weak hinges with sturdier ones and install a deadbolt. You may also want to install a peep-hole so you can keep the door shut until you know who's behind it. If you have any glass panels in your door, these can be covered with grills to improve security. If you want to up your game even more, you can install a security bar or a door jammer. If you opt for a barricade bar, you have an added advantage if the emergency is due to a hurricane: They're great for strengthening your door against high winds.

If you wanted to replace your doors altogether, you could consider security doors (also known as storm doors). Not only do these make it harder for intruders to enter, but they also offer protection from extreme weather.

What we're mostly thinking about here is the standard outside door, but there's a high chance these aren't the only kind of doors you have. If you have sliding glass doors, you automatically have a weak spot in your security system. These can be very easy to open unless you put measures in place to strengthen them. There are a few things you can do to improve the situation, though. You can fit track locks in the base track, or double-bolt locks to prevent the doors from being lifted from their tracks. You could also add sliding locks at the top and bottom of each door. Of course, no matter how many locks you add, glass can always be broken, so you can't completely protect a glass door from intruders. You could consider applying security window film to the glass, though, which will provide a little extra protection.

Securing Windows

Windows are just as vulnerable as glass doors, and they can easily be pried open or broken. The simplest thing you can do is keep them locked when you're out, but you may want to consider some additional reinforcements. Window locks are fairly cheap and come suited for most window types. Be cautious about ones that require a key though because this could slow you down if you need to escape your home in a hurry. Opt instead for sash locks and window latches if possible. If you have horizontal sliding windows, you can improve their security by putting a wooden dowel inside the track. Beyond this, consider what windows allow you to do: They allow you to see out, and therefore, they allow others to see in. Keep your curtains drawn after dark and add blinds in the garage and hallways—areas where you may not be using curtains for comfort.

If you're considering bigger renovations, storm windows are an option. They provide insulation benefits too, which could be a big advantage if the grid goes down, and are helpful against strong winds. You could also consider installing roll-away shutters, but bear in mind that many of these require power. You could also add window grills or bars, but these could cause you problems if you need to exit in an emergency.

Securing Valuables

Hopefully, your deterrents and security measures will keep intruders safely outside, but in the event that someone does make it into your home, it's worth making sure your valuables are protected. One thing you can do is engrave valuable objects with your name and driver's license number, which will deter thieves from taking them. You can also think about where you store your valuables. Most thieves will look in the master bedroom, so consider less appealing places to store things of high value: places like the bathroom or linen closet. It's a good idea to store them inside something that also serves as a decoy too... For example, I've got some of my mother's silver stored in an old coffee tin and stacked in a cupboard. I'm fairly confident that if someone broke in, they'd never know it was even there. For sensitive items like documents, cash, prescription medications, or firearms, opt for a fireproof safe.

The reality, however, is that in an emergency situation, one of your most valuable resources is not your grandmother's jewelry, it's your food stocks. Keep your pantry locked, and if possible, make it look as little like food storage as you can. The likelihood of someone breaking into your home is fairly low, and I certainly don't want you to panic about the safety of your supplies, but I do think it's worth taking measures to protect it—just in case the worst happens.

Firearms

I did touch on firearms briefly in *When Crisis Hits Suburbia*. They're a useful tool to have, both for hunting and for protecting your home, but I think that protecting your family is the most important thing. You're not prepared to lose a single member of your family; therefore, it's important not to operate as a household that's prepared to exchange gunfire. If you keep firearms, keep them safely locked away, and think of them not as a weapon but as a defense you can fall back on only if it is necessary... and also as a way to snag yourself a rabbit for the pot. The last thing I want to say is that if you do find that you need to use a gun to protect your property, bear in mind that your shot doesn't have to be lethal. You can keep someone out of your home without killing them. In fact, some people even switch their ammunition for rock salt, which is an old trick used by farmers to wound an intruder, allowing them to escape without any lasting damage.

The good thing about grid-down security is that it's really not that different from security with the power on. The only things you'll need to rethink are lights and alarms that are wired up to the grid. Everything else you're doing to secure your home is most likely going to be unaffected by a lack of power. That said, extreme weather events could interfere with some of your measures, so be careful to repair anything that is damaged by a flood or storm.

TAKE ACTION: PLAN YOUR ESCAPE ROUTES

To me, defending your home boils down to this: You want to keep your family safe. Therefore, I think a crucial part of security is having a clear idea of how to escape your home in an emergency, be that because of fire or because there's an intruder inside. Use the checklist below to come up with an emergency escape plan. Make sure everyone in the household is familiar with it, and practice it regularly to make sure everyone knows exactly what to do.

ESCAPE ROUTE CHECKLIST

- Identify at least two escape routes from each room in your home
- Clear access to all windows and doors that will be used in an escape
- For multiple-story homes, consider installing escape ladders
- If you have door and window keys, make sure everyone knows where they're kept and ensure that they're accessible in an emergency
- Identify the safest place in the home to hide if escape isn't possible
- Plan for how infants, elderly family members, and pets will be helped out in an emergency
- Come up with a meeting point a safe distance from your home
- Make sure your address is visible on the outside of your property (this will help first responders find you and your home if necessary)
- Practice the escape plan with the whole family (from each room in the house)

IN THE EVENT OF ECONOMIC COLLAPSE

A lot of people ask me about how to prepare for an economic collapse so I wanted to make sure we touched on this topic, but it's important to acknowledge that it could be a whole book in itself. The reality is that there's no way of knowing exactly what will happen if the grid goes down indefinitely, but we can take a few precautions to help us out if things take a turn for the worse.

WHAT'S VALUABLE NOW: CASH

We can only assume that cash will continue to be valuable, at least in the short-term, and it certainly makes little sense to assume that a crisis will mean it will no longer be important. I'd recommend having a supply of cash stashed away safely to see you through a short to medium-term grid-down situation. If the grid is down, ATMs won't work, card readers won't work, and you won't be able to pay for anything online. The banking networks will be down, and in all likelihood, the banks themselves will close. But cash will still have value, and you may need it.

If you need to bug out, you may still be able to buy food or gas, at least in the short-term, or you may be able to buy goods from another household. And if you're sheltering in place, cash could still be useful for buying supplies while they last. Electronic systems may be down, but while there's stock to sell, retailers will want to sell it, so cash is going to be important.

So that brings us to the question of how much cash to have on hand. I'd shoot for something in the region of $1,000–$2,000 to cover last-minute essentials. You should already have stocked your pantry and stored fuel and supplies to see you through a crisis, so unless you're planning on leaving the country (which could be impossible anyway), there really isn't a need for much more than this.

The other thing you'll need to think about is where you're going to store your cash. I think a locked safe somewhere in your home is a good idea: It's somewhere that you can also store important documents, firearms, and any other sensitive items that you don't want to fall into the wrong hands. Other people prefer objects with hidden compartments (like wall clocks or a hidden drawer in a trinket box). What I would say, however, is that it would be wise to store your cash in a waterproof pouch before you put it into any container. If you've been affected by flooding or other extreme weather events, this will help make sure your money's still of use to you.

IF CASH LOSES ITS VALUE

If we find ourselves in a long-term crisis, cash may well lose its value, and if this happens, bartering may become necessary. It's impossible to predict with any certainty what items will be of value if this happens but it's fairly safe to assume that all of your supplies will be highly sought-after items.

What I imagine may become currency in an emergency situation are things that are essential to living, luxury items, or items that act as substitutes for money. In the money substitution category, that might be things like semi-precious metals, silver, or precious stones—things of high value that can be exchanged for necessities. Luxury items might include alcohol, medicine, herbs and spices, sugar, and comfort items (anything from musical instruments to cosmetic products). Beyond this, anything you might need for survival will be of great value: water, food, candles, oil, matches and lighters, ammunition, seeds, salt, batteries, wood, livestock... Anything you might need to keep your family safe and healthy will be what's important to everyone else too.

So what does this mean for you? In terms of things that may eventually become a new form of currency, it means keeping these items safe and well-protected. Jewelry, furs, and any precious metals you have at home could one day be used in exchange for useful resources, so keep these safe. Everything else, you'll only really know about when you get there. If you have a surplus of propane, for example, but your family is short on batteries, you may be able to exchange with someone else to help keep both households stocked. It's another strong argument for conserving resources: Not only will they be essential to your day-to-day life; they might also be valuable currency.

BARTERING TIPS

We live in a currency-based economy, and the chances are you haven't had to do much bartering up to now. Bartering is simply a way of exchanging goods or services, which might involve agreeing to exchange a certain amount of gas for a set quantity of pasta (for example) or agreeing that your neighbor can share your vegetable patch in exchange for them allowing you to pick fruit from their apple trees.

Bartering does come with some risks, however, and therefore, it's best done with people you trust. The problem is, it requires you to disclose something about the supplies you have, and if the person you're talking to turns out to be untrustworthy, this could put your resources—and your home—at risk. This is particularly dangerous if you're trading with addictive substances like alcohol, prescription medications, or tobacco. In these instances, you may be dealing with someone who has an addiction, and this can bring with it extra dangers to your security and safety. The other danger is that trading too much of something you have in your supply closet could mean you don't have it for yourself when you need it later.

Being prepared to barter is a wise move, and a good way to do this is to find out what your friends and neighbors might need. Do they have a particular love of something that you have in abundance? Do you have skills that they lack that you could offer? I think skills are a great way to make trades if you do have to barter because you lose nothing but your time, and only stand to gain valuable additions to your stockpile. Everything from plumbing skills to gardening skills to massage skills could be valuable—so encourage your family to train up and explore their interests. My youngest son is a big animal lover (he once brought an injured duckling home to take care of), and I'm sure he'd be up for training a neighbor's dog in our backyard in exchange for supplies. Everyone's skills are valuable—no matter how young they are.

It's impossible to predict for certain what any future currency might be based on, but my gut feeling is that useful survival items will be the most desirable if currency loses its value. Make sure you have enough cash to see you through a short-term crisis but remember that bartering may become essential further down the line. My goal, however, is to make my family as self-reliant as possible so that we can reduce the chances of this being necessary.

***

TAKE ACTION: DIY DRY BAG

Keeping cash and other valuables safe is about more than security: It's also about protecting it from the environment, and in a serious emergency situation, it's quite likely that this will be necessary. You can make your own dry bag with fairly minimal skills—but who knows? Maybe those skills will be useful for bartering—take the opportunity to practice them!

What You Need

- Strong, waterproof fabric (e.g. Cordura fabric)
- Lighter/seam sealer
- Firm plastic (e.g., plastic from soda bottle)
- Webbing
- Side-release buckle (plastic)
- Polyester thread
- Sewing machine
- Clips to hold the fabric (use clips rather than pins because it's important that the bag doesn't have holes in it)

The Mission

Step 1

Measure and cut out an 8-inch circle on your fabric. The outer inch of this is for seam allowance. Then cut out a 22 x 26-inch rectangle (this will wrap around the circumference of the circle, with an additional inch for seam allowance).

Step 2

Sew the ends of your rectangle together with the fabric inside out, forming a tube. Next, sew the tube onto the circle of fabric, keeping the inside of the fabric facing the tube.

Step 3

Using a lighter or seam sealer, carefully melt the circumference of the base and the length of the body in order to melt the seam and form an airtight seal.

Step 4

Lie the bag down flat so that the seam is in the center and line the plastic up with the top edge of the bag. Cut this down to fit the edge. Now, fold down the top 2 inches of the bag and sew this down. Slide the plastic strip into the resulting pocket.

Step 5

The length of the top of the bag should now be 10 inches. Cut a length of webbing to 20 inches, and sew the side-release buckle on. You'll need part of the buckle at either end, with about 9.5 inches between the two pieces. Now, sew the webbing straps together so that it fits the top of the bag. Sew the strap to the bag on the side opposite the one with the plastic strip.

Step 6

Cut out a hole beneath each end of the buckle to allow it to slide through (your bag is still inside out—when the pieces slide through, they'll be on the outside of the bag).

Step 7

Turn the bag inside out and sew down the buckles on the outside. Roll down the plastic edge a few times to seal it and then clip the buckles together. This should keep your valuables safe from the weather.

NOW FOR THE BEST PART!

You get to help our community by giving this book a review.

Many preppers, just like you, know how hard it is to find current, concise, and useful information, especially when starting. Not only will your review help them on their prepping journey, but the information you direct them to might also save their lives!

Do another prepper a favor and leave a review talking about the information you found, what you liked about the book, and how it helped you... even if it just a sentence or two!

Customer Reviews

★★★★★ 2
5.0 out of 5 stars ▾

5 star		100%
4 star		0%
3 star		0%
2 star		0%
1 star		0%

See all verified purchase reviews ›

Share your thoughts with other customers

Write a customer review ⬅

I am so very appreciative of your review, as it truly makes a difference in our community.

Thank you from the bottom of my heart for purchasing this book. I hope our paths cross again in the future.

Scan this QR code and leave a brief review on Amazon.

CONCLUSION

I sincerely hope we're never in a situation so serious that the grid goes down for a significant length of time. However, there's no denying that it's a possibility, and I think it's important that we prepare for the worst. The more self-reliant you can make your home, the better off you'll be in any emergency situation. The ideal scenario would be to operate completely off the grid, but the reality is that this simply isn't an attainable goal for most families to reach quickly.

If you're new to the preparedness game, the first thing you'll need to do is make sure your pantry is fully stocked (my book, *The Prepper's Pantry*, will help with this), but bear in mind that an emergency situation is likely to take you off-grid, at least for a while. To be fully prepared, you're going to need to be able to cope without municipal power lines. Take an inventory of your current situation and look at what you need to improve on. All of this can be done one step at a time, so approach it methodically and don't panic if it seems like a lot. Every single thing you do to prepare your home for disaster brings you one step closer to the ultimate goal. Being prepared is a journey, and there's pleasure to be found in achieving each small goal.

It still concerns me that so few people are prepared for a grid-down scenario. The chances are this is what will happen in the event of any large-scale emergency. So I have two missions right now: One is to continue to improve my own homestead and take my family one step closer to complete self-reliance each day. And the other is to help other families to do the same. And that's where I'd like to ask you to help me. The more people we can share this information with the better... And how can we do that? We can spread the word. So, if you could spare just five minutes before you start building your earth oven or crafting your first crossbow, leaving a review on Amazon would be a massive help. Think of it as a kind of risk-free bartering: You'll get the satisfaction of sharing your opinion, and in exchange, they'll get their hands on the information they need. Alright, so it's a bit of a stretch, but we all have to help each other here—after all, this isn't the kind of education you get at school.

I'll leave you with one last thought: No matter what happens, stay healthy, stay strong, stay prepared!

Would your family survive in lockdown if society were to collapse? Learn how to prepare your home now.

We are used to a world in which our homes are supplied with fresh water, gas, and electricity.

We're used to having our waste removed and our sanitary needs met.

These are all things we've come to expect, but what would happen if they were taken away?

Flooding, hurricanes, and pandemics are affecting areas we once thought were safe from disaster--we shouldn't take anything for granted.

In *When Crisis Hits Suburbia: A Modern-Day Prepping Guide to Effectively Bug In and Protect Your Family Home in a Societal Collapse,* you'll learn exactly what you need to know to prepare your home for an emergency. You'll find:

- The **6 key priorities of survival** and how to make sure you have them covered

- A clear guide for knowing when it's time to stay in, and when it's time to evacuate
- Top prepper **survival secrets** so that you always stay one step ahead of the rest
- A toolbox of information that allows you to choose what works best for your family
- **Practical tips** for preparing your children for worst-case scenarios without frightening them
- How to make sure your water supply is 100% safe at all times
- Comprehensive checklists for everything you need to stock in your home
- **Essential administrative tasks** you should have sorted in advance before a disaster strikes

And much more.

The ideal home is not only the home that keeps you and your family safe in good times, but it's the home that **keeps you safe no matter what**.

Prepare your home for the worst-case scenario and protect your family no matter what.

Do you know how to stay healthy in the face of an emergency? Prepare now to keep your immune system on your side, no matter what happens tomorrow.

The chances of being stuck in our homes for long periods of time are greater than ever, and when disaster strikes, it can be difficult to get hold of crucial supplies.

Preppers have been evangelizing about food preservation and stockpiling for years. It turns out **they were right**, and now it's time to learn their secrets.

In *The Prepper's Pantry: Nutritional Bulk Food Prepping to Maintain a Healthy Diet and a Strong Immune System to Survive Any Crisis,* you'll find a **comprehensive guide** to preparing for good health in the face of an emergency. You'll discover:

- The **#1 way to stay healthy**, no matter what disaster is thrown your way
- Solid nutritional foundations for good health and strong immunity
- The importance of immune health in the event of an emergency

- 4 crucial food preparation **techniques** you'll need to adopt in order to stock your pantry efficiently
- A fool-proof guide to shopping, preparing, and storing your stocks for safe-keeping
- What **cupboard essentials** you should get a hold of now, and how to prolong their shelf-life
- **Lost skills** previous generations had down to a fine art, yet how you can pick these up once again

And much more.

You won't just be preparing to survive: **you'll be preparing to thrive**.

Know exactly how to prepare for good health in the face of a crisis.

If you haven't already, don't forget to access your free
Emergency Information Planner

Follow the link below to receive your copy:
www.tedrileyauthor.com
Or by accessing the QR code:

You can also join our Facebook community **Suburban Prepping with Ted**, or contact me directly via ted@tedrileyauthor.com.

REFERENCES

Akart, B. (n.d.). *Hygiene sanitation for preppers*. Freedom Preppers. https://www.freedompreppers.com/hygiene-sanitation.htm

Ashworth, B. (2020, July 30). *How to DIY your own hand sanitizer*. Wired. https://www.wired.com/story/how-to-make-hand-sanitizer/

Barton, J. (2022, January 15). *Grid-down communication methods*. The Survival Corps. https://www.thesurvivalcorps.com/grid-down-communication-methods/

Berrie, T. (2020). *How to cook on a wood heat stove*. Our Tiny Homestead. https://www.ourtinyhomestead.com/wood-stove-cooking.html

Blackout: What to do when the grid goes down. (2021, February 19). American Outdoor Guide. https://www.

americanoutdoor.guide/prepping/blackout-what-to-do-when-the-grid-goes-down/

Bleach storage and expiration tips for preppers. (2021, March 11). happypreppers.com. https://www.happypreppers.com/bleach.html

Boechler, E., Hanania, J., Pletnyova, A., Stenhouse, K., Yyelland, B., & Donev, J. (2021, September 27). *Solar chimney.* Energy Education. https://energyeducation.ca/encyclopedia/Solar_chimney

Brady, H. (2018, August 28). *This man has lived off the grid for 20 years—Here's how.* National Geographic. https://www.nationalgeographic.co.uk/environment/2018/08/man-has-lived-grid-20-years-heres-how

Brown, B. (2021, November 22). *Grid down scenarios: How to survive a power grid attack.* The Prepping Guide. https://thepreppingguide.com/grid-down-scenario-causes/

Bryant, C. (2008, July 10). *How radiant floor heating works.* HowStuffWorks. https://home.howstuffworks.com/home-improvement/construction/materials/radiant-floor-heating.htm

Bug out cookware. (2015, August 12). Bug Out Bag Builder. https://www.bugoutbagbuilder.com/product-reviews/bug-out-cookware

Carter, B. (2014, October 28). *Prepper emergency lighting: The best options.* US Preppers. Be Prepared, Not Scared.

https://uspreppers.com/prepper-emergency-lighting-the-best-options/

Centers, J. (2021, January 23). *Best emergency candles.* The Prepared. https://theprepared.com/gear/reviews/candles/

Cobb, J. (2014, November 14). *Using water heater water in an emergency.* The Survival Mom. https://thesurvivalmom.com/water-heater-emergency-water-supply/

Coffman, S. (2021, December 23). *5 ways to contact loved ones after the grid goes down.* Urban Survival Site. https://urbansurvivalsite.com/ways-contact-loved-ones-grid-goes/

Creekmore, M. D. (2019, October 21). *What are the best alternative heat sources to use during a power outage?* MDCreekmore.com. https://mdcreekmore.com/staying-warm-and-heating-your-home-during-a-long-term-grid-down-situation/

Denzer, K. (2002, October 1). *Build your own wood-fired earth oven.* Mother Earth News. https://www.motherearthnews.com/diy/build-your-own-wood-fired-earth-oven-zmaz02onzgoe/

Deziel, C. W. (2022, January 31). *What is a solar fan? (with pictures).* WiseGeek. https://www.wise-geek.com/what-is-a-solar-fan.htm

Dodrill, T. (2021, December 21). *20 SHTF currency options better than gold.* Survival Sullivan. https://www.survivalsullivan.com/shtf-currency-options-better-gold/

Dunn, C. (2020, September 29). *Generating off-grid power: The 4 best ways.* Treehugger. https://www.treehugger.com/generating-off-grid-power-the-four-best-ways-4858714

8 different types of generators for your off-the-grid cabin. (2021, August 20). Architecture Lab. https://www.architecturelab.net/types-of-generators/

Engels, J. (2017, January 16). *How to make a hot water heater with compost.* One Green Planet. https://www.onegreenplanet.org/lifestyle/hot-water-heater-with-compost/

5 effective ways to heat your home during a power outage. (2020, September 28). The Prepping Guide. https://theppreppingguide.com/heat-your-home-during-power-outage/

Fortey, I. (2020, August 23). *How to make a dry bag.* Boat Safe. https://www.boatsafe.com/how-to-make-a-dry-bag/

Garen, J. R. (2021, December 21). *Emergency lighting solutions for preppers.* DIY Prepper. https://www.diyprepper.com/emergency-lighting-solutions-for-preppers/

Garen, J. R. (2021, December 21). *How do preppers store water? Storage ideas and solutions.* DIY Prepper. https://www.diyprepper.com/prepper-water-storage/

Geothermal energy: Mother Nature's HVAC. (2020, January 29). American Outdoor Guide. https://www.americanoutdoor.guide/survival-gear/survival-gear-guides/geothermal-energy-101/

Hart, N. (2020, August 27). *How to make a solar panel emergency backup system.* Dengarden. https://dengarden.com/safety/How-To-Make-A-Solar-Panel-Emergency-Backup-System

Hart, S. (2016, January 15). *Hurricane lantern old school preppers light.* UK Preppers Guide. https://www.ukpreppersguide.co.uk/hurricane-lantern-old-school-preppers-light/

Heating and cooling an off-grid home. (2021, June 25). Survival Realty. https://www.survivalrealty.com/2021/06/25/heating-and-cooling-an-off-grid-home/?utm_source=rss&utm_medium=rss&utm_campaign=heating-and-cooling-an-off-grid-home

Heddings, J. (2019, September 9). *The best emergency/camping LED lanterns.* Review Geek. https://www.reviewgeek.com/20642/the-best-emergency-camping-led-lanterns/

Henry, P. (2013, February 26). *Where there is no kitchen: Cooking when the grid goes down.* The Prepper Journal.

https://theprepperjournal.com/2013/02/26/where-there-is-no-kitchen-cooking-when-the-grid-goes-down/

Henry, P. (2013, September 7). *Medicine to stock up on for when there is no doctor.* The Prepper Journal. https://theprepperjournal.com/2015/09/07/medicine-to-stock-up-on/

Henry, P. (2013, November 8). *Do you have water if the grid goes down?* The Prepper Journal. https://theprepperjournal.com/2013/11/08/water-if-the-grid-goes-down/

Henry, P. (2015, April 28). *How much cash should you have if the grid goes down?* The Prepper Journal. https://theprepperjournal.com/2015/04/28/how-much-cash-should-you-have-if-the-grid-goes-down/

Herbst, C. (2022, January 27). *17 power outage supplies you need in case of an emergency.* Taste of Home. https://www.tasteofhome.com/collection/power-outage-supplies/

How do propane heaters work. (2022, January 16). Home Air Guides. https://homeairguides.com/how-do-propane-heaters-work

Howell, B. (2021, October 26). *A step-by-step guide to going off-grid.* The Eco Experts. https://www.theecoexperts.co.uk/blog/going-off-grid

How to make a crossbow. (2020, July 25). wikiHow. Retrieved February 10, 2022, from https://www.wikihow.com/Make-a-Crossbow

How to make a solar oven. (2022). Education.com. https://www.education.com/science-fair/article/design-solar-cooker/

How to plan your emergency escape route. (n.d.). First Alert. https://www.firstalert.com/on/demandware.store/Sites-firstalert-Site/default/Content-Show?cid=escape-plan

How to wash dishes while camping. (2019, October 26). Fresh Off The Grid. https://www.freshoffthegrid.com/washing-dishes-while-camping/

James, J. (2021, December 30). *4 steps to building the best fire pits in survival shelters.* Survival Freedom. https://survivalfreedom.com/building-the-best-fire-pits-in-survival-situations-based-on-shelter-type/

Johnson, J. (2018, August 31). *4 ways to wash clothes on your off-grid homestead.* Down to Earth Homesteaders. https://downtoearthhomesteaders.com/4-ways-to-wash-clothes-on-your-off-grid-homestead/

Jones, K. (2018, August 11). *Prepping for basic emergency sanitation.* The Provident Prepper. https://theprovidentprepper.org/prepping-for-basic-emergency-sanitation/

Jones, K. (2019, April 9). *The prepper's guide to securing your home.* The Provident Prepper. https://theprovidentprepper.org/the-preppers-guide-to-securing-your-home/

Jones, K. (2019, July 10). *Prepper home pharmacy: The best medications to stockpile.* The Provident Prepper. https://theprovidentprepper.org/prepper-home-pharmacy-the-best-medications-to-stockpile/

Jones, K. (2019, October 18). *A wise prepper's guide to bartering skills and supplies.* The Provident Prepper. https://theprovidentprepper.org/a-wise-preppers-guide-to-bartering-skills-and-supplies/

Jones, K. (2019, December 5). *30 day grid-down cooking challenge—Lessons learned and fuel usage.* The Provident Prepper. https://theprovidentprepper.org/30-day-grid-down-cooking-challenge-lessons-learned-and-fuel-usage/

Jones, K. (2020, October 23). *6 lifesaving tips to keep warm during a winter power outage.* The Provident Prepper. https://theprovidentprepper.org/6-lifesaving-tips-to-keep-warm-during-a-winter-power-outage/

Jones, K. (2021, August 7). *7 lifesaving tips to help you survive a summer power outage.* The Provident Prepper. https://theprovidentprepper.org/7-lifesaving-tips-to-help-you-survive-a-summer-power-outage/

Jones, K., & Jones, J. (n.d.). *Emergency heating—Recommended products*. The Provident Prepper. https://theprovidentprepper.org/recommended-products/emergency-heating-recommended-products/

Jones, M. (2021, March 22). *Camp cooking: How to cook over a campfire*. advnture.com. https://www.advnture.com/how-to/cook-over-a-campfire

Kenneth. (2020, March 4). *Preparing for grid down: My step-by-step to-do list*. The Provident Prepper. https://theprovidentprepper.org/preparing-for-grid-down-my-step-by-step-to-do-list/

Lampert, E. (2019, May 22). *Off-grid power systems: 7 main types and the safety components you'll need*. Green Building Canada. https://greenbuildingcanada.ca/2019/off-grid-living/

Larsen, J. (2020, August 11). *How much water should a dog drink?* PetMD. https://www.petmd.com/dog/nutrition/evr_dg_the_importance_of_water

MacWelch, T. (2016, February 3). *How to build your own reflecting oven for camping or survival situations*. Outdoor Life. https://www.outdoorlife.com/blogs/survivalist/how-build-your-own-reflecting-oven-camping-or-survival-situations/

Margene. (2021, January 26). *DIY cooking without electricity*. DIY Preparedness. https://diypreparedness.net/diy-cooking-without-electricity/

McCafferty, E. (2019, July 17). *Keep your house cool without air conditioning.* Accidental Hippies. https://www.accidentalhippies.com/house-cool-without-air-conditioning/

McCoy, S. (2021, December 16). *The best flashlights of 2022.* GearJunkie. https://gearjunkie.com/outdoor/hiking/best-flashlights

McLean, J. (n.d.). *The most effective off grid home heating methods.* Thermal Earth. https://www.thermalearth.co.uk/blog/most-effective-off-grid-home-heating-methods

MissouriVillian. (2011, September 21). *7 methods of primitive fire starting.* Instructables. https://www.instructables.com/7-Methods-of-Primitive-Fire-Starting/

"Mountain Man" John. (2015, June 10). *Distilling—An overlooked survival skill.* Intrepid Outdoors. https://intrepidoutdoors.com/distilling-overlooked-survival-skill/

Muhjesbude, M. (n.d.). *10 must have alternative remedies for preppers.* https://www.survivopedia.com/must-have-alternative-remedies-for-preppers/

National Academies of Sciences, Engineering, and Medicine. (2017). *Enhancing the resilience of the nation's electricity system.* National Academies Press. https://doi.org/10.17226/24836

Natural herbs and plants for medicine and illness that you should be storing. (2019, February 20). UK Preppers Guide. https://www.ukpreppersguide.co.uk/natural-herbs-and-plants-for-medicine-and-illness-that-you-should-be-storing/

Nicholas O. (2014, October 21). *4 life-saving ways to communicate when the power is out.* Off The Grid News. https://www.offthegridnews.com/extreme-survival/4-life-saving-ways-to-communicate-when-the-power-is-out/

Oetken, N. (2017, November 5). *How to communicate when the grid goes down.* Outdoor Revival. https://www.outdoorrevival.com/instant-articles/communicate-grid-goes.html?chrome=1

Off grid. (2022, February 10). Energy Saving Trust. https://energysavingtrust.org.uk/advice/off-grid/

Planning an escape. (2021, July 2). NI Direct. https://www.nidirect.gov.uk/articles/planning-escape

Rader, T. (2019, June 15). *IFAK first aid kit list.* The Prepared. https://theprepared.com/bug-out-bags/guides/first-aid-kit-list/

Ramey, J. (2021, May 7). *Best headlamps for prepping.* The Prepared. https://theprepared.com/gear/reviews/headlamps/

Ready, J. (2020, June 19). *9 quick and efficient ways to wash clothes without electricity.* Ready Lifestyle. https://readylifestyle.com/how-to-wash-clothes-without-electricity/

Rejba, A. (2022, January 11). *9 methods to start a fire without matches or lighter.* The Smart Survivalist Blog. https://www.thesmartsurvivalist.com/9-methods-to-start-a-fire-without-matches-or-lighter/

Rhoades, J. (2021, July 23). *Using rain barrels: Learn about collecting rainwater for gardening.* Gardening Know How. https://www.gardeningknowhow.com/garden-how-to/watering/collecting-rainwater.htm

Rich M. (2015, September 30). *The 7 most important survival skills when the grid's down.* Off The Grid News. https://www.offthegridnews.com/extreme-survival/the-7-most-important-survival-skills-when-the-grids-down/

Rich M. (2016, January 12). *3 emergency heat sources when the power's out.* Off The Grid News. https://www.offthegridnews.com/grid-threats/3-emergency-heat-sources-when-the-powers-out/

Riley, T. (2021). *When crisis hits suburbia: A modern-day prepping guide to effectively bug in and protect your family home in a societal collapse.*

Should you get a kerosene or propane portable heater? (2020, October 28). Mi-T-M Blog. https://www.mitm.com/blog/get-kerosene-propane-portable-heater/

Siler, W. (2015, May 20). *How to build the only five campfires you'll ever need.* Gizmodo. https://gizmodo.com/how-to-build-the-only-five-campfires-you-ll-ever-need-1705895804

Stewart, C. (2021, June 1). *Power's out and in a pinch? How to create 5 makeshift urban survival lights.* The Art of Manliness. https://www.artofmanliness.com/skills/outdoor-survival/powers-out-and-in-a-pinch-how-to-create-5-makeshift-urban-survival-lights/

Storing energy. (2022, February 10). Energy Saving Trust. https://energysavingtrust.org.uk/advice/storing-energy/

Storing salt for survival. (2021, February 1). happypreppers.com. https://www.happypreppers.com/salt.html

Superfood for survival | How to make stinging nettle tea. (2020, April 5). UK Preppers Guide. https://www.ukpreppersguide.co.uk/superfood-for-survival-how-to-make-stinging-nettle-tea/

Survival medicine for grid down survival. (n.d.). Family Survival Planning. https://www.familysurvivalplanning.com/survival-medicine.html

Survival sanitation: How to deal with human waste. (2019, February 25). The Prepper Journal. https://theprepperjournal.com/2014/03/17/how-to-deal-with-human-waste/

Tate, A. (2020, December 27). *Emergency radio frequencies preppers must know*. SHTF Blog. https://www.shtfblog. com/emergency-radio-frequencies-preppers-must-know/

Tips for basic backup power in a power outage or a SHTF situation. (2021, November 16). The Village Prepper. https:// thevillageprepper.com/tips-for-basic-backup-power-in-a-power-outage-or-a-shtf-situation/

Top 7 emergency light sources for preppers. (2022, February 9). The City Dark. https://thecitydark.com/top-7-emergency-light-sources-for-preppers/

12 must have items for an emergency power out. (2019, October 1). Magic Valley Electric. https://www. electricteam.com/blog/2019/october/12-must-have-items-for-an-emergency-power-out/

Vuković, D. (2021, May 27). *22 ways to cook without electricity when the grid fails*. Primal Survivor. https://www. primalsurvivor.net/ways-cook-without-electricity/

Vuković, D. (2021, August 30). *Essential survival lights and lighting: 9 options for disaster preparedness*. Primal Survivor. https://www.primalsurvivor.net/survival-lighting/

Walter, J. (2018, August 6). *Foraging for food in a winter survival situation*. Super Prepper. https://www. superprepper.com/foraging-for-food-in-a-winter-survival-situation/

WaterBob vs AquaPod: Bathtub storage made easy. (2021, June 3). Primal Survivor. https://www.primalsurvivor.net/waterbob-vs-aquapod/

Water survival guide. (2021, March 31). happypreppers.-com. https://www.happypreppers.com/water.html

What is biogas? (n.d.). National Grid Group. https://www.nationalgrid.com/stories/energy-explained/what-is-biogas

Why is propane stored in household tanks but natural gas is not. (2019, August 22). Dependable LP Gas Company. https://www.dependablelpgas.com/why-is-propane-stored-in-household-tanks-but-natural-gas-is-not/

Williams College. (n.d.). *Passive solar design.* Sustainability. https://sustainability.williams.edu/green-building-basics/passive-solar-design/

WINDExchange. (n.d.). *Small wind guidebook.* US Department of Energy. https://windexchange.energy.gov/small-wind-guidebook